Casualties of Privilege

Essays on Prep Schools' Hidden Culture

Edited by
Louis M. Crosier

1991
AVOCUS PUBLISHING, INC.
WASHINGTON, D.C.

CASUALTIES OF PRIVILEGE:
ESSAYS ON PREP SCHOOLS' HIDDEN CULTURE

Published by:

Avocus Publishing, Inc.
1223 Potomac Street, N.W.
Washington, D.C. 20007 U.S.A.
Telephone: 202-333-8190
Fax: 202-337-3809

Disclaimer:

Nothing contained in this book is intended in any way to be libelous in nature. Neither is it the intent of Avocus Publishing, Inc. to publish any accusatory statement, direct or implied, of improper motives or illegal actions by any individual or educational institution. Any other interpretation of our printing is erroneous and therefore misunderstood. We believe that the public interest in general, and education in particular, will be better served by the publication of the authors' experiences. All names of individuals and prep schools have been changed or omitted.

Library of Congress Catalog Card Number: 90-084618

ISBN 0-9627671-0-7: $14.95 Softcover

10 9 8 7 6 5 4 3
First printing March 1991
Second printing May 1991
Third printing July 1991

Cover design by Sharon Oleksiak

For Claire
An Exceptional Educator
and
A True Optimist

Acknowledgements

In the three years since the start of this project, I have had a great deal of help from a varied and creative group of advisors, contributors, and volunteers from all corners of the prep school world. I have never yet experienced a team effort so great, and I thank everyone who worked to bring this endeavor to its final product.

Several people, in particular, have affected my work on this project and, more broadly, my work as a teacher. I hope to pass on their inspiration through additional group efforts which promote school improvement and healthy education as this one seeks to do. A great deal is owed to Janet Eisendrath with whom I have had the honor of interacting on several levels — as a student, colleague, and friend. Her wisdom and indefatigable respect for young people is an example for anyone who works with children. Eric Rofes and The Fayerweather Street School planted the seed for group authorship by providing me and my lower-school classmates with the opportunity to take an experience common to many of us and present it from a new perspective. The result was *The Kids' Book of Divorce*.

In addition to the prime movers, many others made this project come to life. Page and Pipe have provided ongoing encouragement and advice concerning publication. Lucinda's creative spirit resuscitated a limp title. Sue Lena's cautionary steering and helpful references taught me the lingo of the trade. The principals and directors of Avocus Publishing, Inc. have provided their patience, support, and enthusiasm from the start. I am most grateful to Robert N. Pyle & Associates for the endless hours of use of office space and equipment. I have also been fortunate to receive many helpful comments from the university community, parents, and boarding school faculty and administrators who were kind enough to share their thoughts with me.

Louis M. Crosier

Contents

Preface

Casualties of Privilege: Essays on Prep Schools' Hidden Culture is a response to concerns I had as a student at boarding school. Subsequently, when I became a member of the residential faculty at the same school, my discussions with students, faculty, and alumni clarified and reinforced my earlier impressions, and led me to the conclusion that most boarding schools in their current form do not promote healthy adolescent development.

My feelings are best captured by the comments made one evening by a student in my dorm. He told me there had been "a lot of strange behavior" on campus, and he felt it was due to the lack of adult role models. He said:

> Since there aren't enough grown-ups around to set the limits, we turn to each other and adopt one another's values. We often lose sight of right from wrong. We get caught up in experimenting and have so little contact with the outside world that we lose perspective on our actions and respond by creating our own behavioral norms and values.

As in *Lord of the Flies,* he felt that the students create a subculture. They establish networks, rituals, and a power structure and learn behavioral facades so the faculty doesn't know what they are really up to.

As the adult responsible for a residence hall, I am so tired by the end of my normal work day that I am not able to give all the young people in my dorm the quality time and attention they require. Now, I can finally understand what was missing from my experience as a prep school student — I didn't get much guidance from grown-ups who could have provided support given that they had already experienced the growing pains felt during the volatile and fragile period of adolescence.

When I reflect back on my experience in high school, I remember feeling inadequate because my behavior was irresponsible and self-defeating. Now, I understand that the structure of the environment played a role in shaping that behavior. In fact, even the adults in the community are not immune to its influence. The strength of a culture is elusive, and most parents and residential faculty are unaware of the extent to which it permeates and controls the children's lives at boarding school.

Casualties of Privilege combines the perspective of seventeen graduates of prestigious New England prep schools. Each writer tells a personal story. Together the essays form a composite picture of the issues students encounter during their years at boarding school. Different from the existing literature on residential schools, written by authorities looking into the system from the outside, *Casualties of Privilege* takes an insider's look at the issues which are beneath the surface of these privileged institutions. Existing work focuses on the superior quality of instruction, curricular offerings and facilities, the geographic and ethnic composition of students and faculty, and the differences between residential schools and their public counterparts. But there is more going on. I hope this additional perspective on boarding life will enhance our understanding of the prep school system and encourage us to improve it.

There is little doubt that prep school students emerge from residential schools with an excellent academic foundation. But a child's intellect should not be a residential school's primary concern. Different from public or day schools, boarding schools must provide their students with the emotional and moral education ordinarily provided by the family. Since these adolescents don't go home at night, who else is going to do it? Despite the lip service school catalogues pay to students' emotional development, it is in this area that prep schools prove weakest. Changes need to be made to create a healthier environment.

Casualties of Privilege is meant to spark reaction and discussion, for it will only be through thoughtful evaluation and appropriate restructuring that prep schools will upgrade their boarding programs. As a supporter of the movement to improve schools, I believe criticism must be accompanied by constructive, viable solutions. Thus, the final chapter of *Casualties of Privilege* seeks to lay the foundation from which prep schools can move toward tackling issues raised in the essays herein. It is my hope that prep schools will continue to strive for intellectual excellence but no longer at the expense of their students' healthy emotional growth. Ultimately, boarding schools can facilitate teenagers' understanding of themselves and enable them to meet their needs responsibly while making constructive contributions to the society for which we are "preparing" them to be leaders.

Louis M. Crosier

Foreword

by Theodore R. Mitchell
Chair
Department of Education
Dartmouth College

Casualties of Privilege is a powerful, indeed unprecedented, look inside the world of elite boarding schools. Insiders, outsiders, black and white, these former students tell their stories of life within the peer culture of some of America's best prep schools. These are stories about drinking, drugs, and sex. They are also stories about friendship, trust, and loyalty. Most of all, they are stories about striving to fit in, about yearning to grow up, and about managing, or mismanaging the extraordinary academic expectations of families, teachers, and society at large.

We are often barraged by statistical summaries that try to reveal changes in the behavior of young adults. This many teen-age pregnancies, that many drop outs . . . these numbers can tell us only so much. Far more profound are the stories told in this volume, stories that help us understand 'why' and 'so what' as well as the 'how many.' The answers to those questions that are found inside *Casualties of Privilege* make me uncomfortable, but I think that was at least a part of their intent.

As a set of stories, the book is compelling and disturbing. It challenges all of us who have an interest in independent schools to attend more closely to the lives of students, and it provides the foundation for a plan to make prep school a healthier environment for teenagers. As a collection, it is a long overdue contribution to the study of residential schools and the intended and unintended effects they have on those who live within them.

It hardly seems possible that it has been thirty years since Erving Goffman first brought into focus the particular attributes of what he called "total institutions," in a book appropriately titled *Asylums: Essays on the Social Situation of Mental Patients and Other Inmates.*[1] Since then, Goffman's analytic framework has been used to illuminate the workings of prisons, mental hospitals, monasteries, and the Marine Corps . . . all, in Goffman's words:

---

[1]Erving Goffman, *Asylums: Essays on the Social Situation of Mental Patients and Other Inmates* (New York: Doubleday and Company, 1961).

places of residence and work where a large number of like situated individuals, cut off from the wider society for an appreciable period of time, together lead an enclosed, formally administered round of life.[2]

It is equally improbable, and far more disturbing, that despite the obvious structural connections, Goffman's powerful analytic tools for the study of total institutions have not until recently been applied to boarding schools . . . either by those who study private schools or by those who run them.[3]

This reflects, I think, a peculiar reluctance to look behind the veil and to analyze with some rigor a set of institutions whose educational prowess and symbolic importance in conferring or confirming social status has achieved mythical proportions in late twentieth century America. It also reflects a rather simplistic, almost visceral reluctance to talk about prep schools in the same sentence as prisons and mental institutions. After all, we all know that prep schools are 'good institutions' and prisons, 'bad.' We reject out-of-hand a discussion that refers to prep school students, some of the brightest and most privileged of society's youth, as "inmates" and that employs analytical models that put them in the company of monks, nuns, jar-heads, and the criminally insane.

Goffman's brilliance was, though, to do just that, to demonstrate that the institutions we establish to treat, educate, indoctrinate, or incarcerate draw from a common palate of organizational features, operate in common ways, and share common outcomes despite the difference in their purposes, their clients, and their social coloring. The issue is not 'good' institutions contrasted to 'bad'; it is, rather, the broadly-supported power of institutions like prisons and prep schools to create and sustain a complete culture in which their goals can be met without the inevitable distractions of the "outside world."

The central element of a complete culture, or a "total institution" is, in Goffman's framework, the erasure of the traditional divisions between work, sleep, and play. Individuals inside total institutions do not migrate between different systems of authority, like family and work, but live within a single framework of rules and relationships. In prep schools, where one teacher fills the roles of instructor (work), coach (play), and dormitory 'parent' (sleep), this unity is especially clear. The real and extraordinary educative power of boarding schools emanates directly from their ability to regulate and direct each aspect of a student's life toward the educational goals of the institution. Lessons learned in the classroom can be reinforced on the playing field and in the dormitory.

---

[2]*Asylums* p. xiii.

[3]Peter Cookson and Caroline Persell, *Preparing for Power: America's Elite Boarding Schools* (New York: Basic Books, 1985) broke new ground in using Goffman's framework but focuses more broadly and at a far greater distance than the current volume.

Total institutions create this congruence in four distinct ways, according to Goffman.[4] First, authority is centralized and exposure to the 'outside' is carefully controlled. Weekend "passes," sign out sheets, and the relative imperviousness of the campus to the 'locals' all reflect this ability of boarding schools to shut themselves and their charges off from the world. Second, individuals are grouped together during the day and activities take place "in the company of others, all of whom are treated alike and required to do the same thing together." Common curfew times, study hall, and formal dinners all send the message to students that they are parts of a whole that is greater than themselves. Third, all phases of the day's activities are tightly scheduled and "the whole sequence of activities is imposed from above by a system of explicit formal rulings." Finally, each aspect of the daily schedule, each activity and each program, is "brought together into a single rational plan purportedly designed to fulfill the official aims of the institution." The result is a tightly woven fabric of activities all designed to create an overpowering and undeniable educational environment, a total institution in which young men and women can't avoid the message of the institution.

What this means for young adolescents transported from the varied worlds of family, neighborhood, school, church, and friendships into the singular world of boarding school is a series of unlearnings and learnings. Old ways are unlearned as new ways are learned. The culture and the logic of the prep school is substituted for the divided cultures of 'the outside world.' New words, new taboos, new rites and rituals of passage mark off the culture of the school from others and at once make initiates feel a part of the culture and apart from their former lives of home and friends. Indeed, as the process of inculturation proceeds, the individual student's sense of self is transformed within a new context of academic, social, and behavioral references.

In the logical world where theory reigns untrammeled, this transformation is controlled and directed down to its smallest detail to cohere with the educational goals of the boarding school. In this world, the norms, habits, and values instilled by life in boarding school are those advertised in so many promotional brochures: intellectual independence, thoughtful action, concern for others, respect for diversity, dedication, perseverance, and self-esteem. In the real world of real institutions and real kids, the transformative power of boarding schools does work to achieve these ends . . . and works remarkably well. At the same time, the hot house that is the boarding school also provides fertile ground for other kinds of transformations, specifically for the creation of a sophisticated student subculture that is at once reflective of and oppositional to the imposed culture of the school. It is this subculture that is the subject of the rich essays collected in *Casualties of Privilege*.

It is easy and tempting to dismiss drug use and rule breaking, two elements of the subculture described in *Casualties of Privilege,* as the aberrant behavior

---

[4]*Asylums* p.6.

of a few maladjusted students. Yet, as these stories reveal, such assumptions are wrong. The student subculture, in both its most positive and most negative faces, emerges as a natural response to the totality of the institution in which students find themselves. It develops as the students strive to take charge and impose their own mark on a life that is controlled by others and marked by rules and restrictions over which they have little influence. To put it even more starkly, as one of the authors does below in talking about drinking, "the idea of breaking rules was at least as exciting and enjoyable as the act itself."[5]

Story after story in *Casualties of Privilege* tells of the elaborate rituals and the refined technologies engineered to "beat the system," passed down from student generation to student generation. After reading these accounts one cannot deny the reality of the student subculture, nor its richness, nor its internal logic . . . nor finally and tragically, its danger.

The creation of a subculture in which status is conferred upon those who "beat the system" is a common feature of all total institutions. Goffman calls them "secondary adjustments," which "allow inmates to obtain forbidden satisfactions or to obtain permitted ones by forbidden means."[6]

In many of its dimensions, the student subculture is harmless, and even develops traits of leadership and initiative which are in other settings prized by the authorities as well as the students. A late night swim, a raid on the dining hall, well-designed pranks . . . these are the light side of the secondary adjustments students make within the boundaries of prep school life. But as *Casualties of Privilege* makes abundantly clear, there is a powerful dark side to the oppositional culture mounted by students in boarding schools. On this dark side, drug use, eating disorders, and sexual activity become more than simply common place . . . they become the common currency of social acceptance and individual prowess. Rule-breakers become legends and models for younger students. The greater the risk, the bigger the legend. Making love in the balcony of the chapel while teachers converse below; this is risk taking for its own sake . . . and for the sake of immortality within the system of myths and legends that define the student subculture.[7]

But even more dangerous and troubling than the linking of social acceptance to destructive behavior is the linking of self-esteem with self-destruction. As one author puts it:

> As a boarding student I felt out of control because it was the institution that set every minute of my daily schedule. My self-destructive behavior and that of my friends was our attempt to establish control over our existence.[8]

---

[5]"Living Inside the Prep Culture," p.9.

[6]*Asylums* p.54.

[7]"Beating the System," p.137.

[8] "Depression," p.55.

It is in this expression of despair that the images of prisoner, inmate, and student do indeed collapse into one. For some, the totality of a total institution is too confining, too restricting of self. Where the institution seeks to nourish, even force feed, it instead chokes and stifles. For these individuals, whether in prison, concentration camps, or boarding schools, the cry for help and for escape is unmistakably linked to the last and most terrible freedom we have, the freedom to destroy our bodies, either quickly or slowly. With stories that shout, laugh, and cry with authenticity, *Casualties of Privilege* flesh out Goffman's framework and provide unique insights into the effects of total institutions on their clients. The real power of *Casualties of Privilege* lies in its ability to guide us through the world of the student subculture, to take us inside the 'walled garden' of the prep school and to help us see it through the eyes of those who live its controlled life, the students.

The stories are honest, sometimes brutally so, and in their intensity they reveal much about the lives of students and the lives of these special institutions. The voices are varied: ranging from celebration to despair. The emotions are authentic: one can feel the pain along with the triumph. Most of all, the line of sight is dead center true: these are young adults telling their own stories in their own words. We must be thankful for their frankness and grateful for the insights they provide.

In the end, the stories are unsettling and their message weighty. Myths explode, Edenic images cloud over with the reality of the lives lived in boarding schools, and we are reminded of the tremendous vulnerability of adolescents, even, or maybe especially in institutions as seemingly complete and comprehensive as the boarding school. Yet there is also a great deal of hope in these stories. For while many of the stories reveal the dark side of student culture, the academic richness, the impact of good teachers, and the grounding in values of friendship and honor, even if misplaced, show at the edges of the stage like characters eager for their cue. Perhaps *Casualties of Privilege* is just that, the cue for the dedicated professionals within these schools, the teachers and headmasters, to join parents and the students themselves in realigning the cultures of the school to a set of shared goals and then in acting upon those goals. If *Casualties of Privilege* simply sparks a new round of crackdowns against drugs and a new restriction of student freedoms, it will have failed. It will have succeeded, however, if it serves as the starting point for a discussion of how to harmonize the power inherent in total institutions with the stated educational goals of the best schools in the land, goals that include not only academic prowess but also personal growth, independent and responsible decision-making, and real leadership.

My guess, and my hope, is that it will succeed!

1

Living Inside the Prep Culture

by Hibberd Melville

What you will see in any boarding school's catalogue will be nice — photographs of boys and girls of all races in various states of exertion and achievement — on bucolic fields, gritting their teeth as they head soccer balls, gazing sternly at sheet music as they draw bows across cellos, or smiling as they de-bug computer programs. It will not show students smoking dope, snorting coke, or doing shots; they make up the reality beneath the shiny surface of prep school life, a surface of seeming perfection which masks threats to students. The prep subculture places a premium on deception. A self-contained court along almost medieval lines, it rewards those who best feign being what they are not, those who conceal lives of quiet debauchery behind a frenzied tapestry of sports, study, and legitimate extracurriculars.

Imagine a little note: "Warning to Parents: There is a certain amount of sex, drug, and alcohol abuse at this school which is beyond our ability to control. School administrators therefore cannot assume responsibility for any damage to life, limb or property ensuing therefrom."

Parents should be aware of the unseen realities and experiences of prep school before sending their kids off. Few parents consider how well they could manage a household of twenty or thirty kids. Invariably, such a large group forms networks to beat the system. In fact, they establish their own system; the inmates take over the asylum.

In the turbulence of the 1970's, my boarding school participated in the national moral restructuring. Nothing was strict or defined anymore. As good and evil became relative terms, students at my school let their hair grow long, started experimenting with psychoactive substances and listening to rebellious music.

The school followed the national trend, dropping most dress code requirements and going co-educational. As the turbulence subsided, school administrators saw they had effected a number of positive changes. But they did not seem aware of the troubling vestiges of the 1960's and 1970's. Because of the insularity of boarding schools, these vestiges have become institutions. "It was a cyclical thing passed down from year to year," said one former student.

It was all "part of the process of defining your own territory as student vs. teacher," he said. The language, the modes of dress, of room decoration, and the drug-related rites of passage can survive for a long time at boarding schools. The way '60's culture survived at my school, ten or twenty years after it had begun to fade everywhere, reminded me of stories of Japanese World War II veterans on Pacific Islands who didn't realize the war was over because they had had no contact with the outside world.

I was fairly naive when I went away to boarding school. I was fifteen and could have passed for twelve. There were people in my class who were shaving and looked like adults. There were people who lived their lives like adults: drinking, having sex and doing all the things traditionally associated with adults, even though they were members of a community that required they do none of these things.

Whatever you may think about kids smoking marijuana and doing other drugs — whether you think it a "recreational" activity or "a plague upon the land," — you wouldn't want to see Drug Abuse listed among the extracurriculars. Or if you did, you probably wouldn't send your kid away to school. Nonetheless, drug use is an integral part of prep school culture. I am not a drug-alarmist; I only say these things happen to students at boarding schools. And because of living and going to school in the same place with the same people, a certain unhealthy attitude develops. It is this attitude, the one that prizes beating the system and creating false appearances, that encourages and governs drug use at boarding schools.

Initiation of younger kids, new boys — "newbs" (a derogatory term formed by the contraction of "new" and "boy") was a mark of seniority. It was through the older students that the culture perpetuated itself. They were the high priests in the rites of passage and taught the younger ones how to get along. "It was a big kick to get somebody stoned. Corruption was the big goal. You know, makes you feel powerful," one student said.

There was such a powerful student in my dormitory my first year at boarding school. He was tall, blond, and healthy-looking. At seventeen, he looked more dashing than any of the young faculty members at our small, New England boarding school. He liked to wear clogs. He did a lot of things which would have gotten people who were less studly in a lot of trouble. And he did them, of course, to prove how sure he was of his self-image.

His ancestry and immediate family embodied enormous power, wealth and prestige, even by prep school standards; you would probably recognize the name as belonging to one of America's oldest and richest families. He played on the soccer team and was an expert skier. Soon he would be named one of the most eligible bachelors in America. That was the surface. Beneath the gloss cover was someone who could intimidate you into doing almost anything, someone who could urinate on you in the shower and hold you there helpless, or pounce on you while you were asleep to feel your embarrassingly hairless armpits. I'll call him "Jones."

In his room, one of the two prized singles in the dorm, he had all the amenities: a stereo, tapestries, drugs and brick-a-brac from an assortment of Third World countries. As new students, we were in awe and terror of this popular student. He was at times our mentor and at others our tormentor. He had a live-in girlfriend. That, of course, was illegal. But it seemed the teachers were as scared of him as we were of his stature, his power, his machismo, his assurance, and his moodiness. I lived in a double room in Jones' dorm, my door about five feet from his. "I grew up on pot," I remember Jones boasting. It struck me as amazing when he said it: first, that he had grown up; he certainly seemed to have (I wondered if I, myself, could ever be so grown up); then, that he saw marijuana as harmless. This evil drug of my childhood nightmares was to him a benevolent herb, something to be lived with and loved.

The first time I ever got stoned, I was almost sixteen. The air had turned cold, and the ponds around the school had grown their first brittle skins of ice. It was October. The leaves were down, and it was still early in the school year. A couple of friends and I were sitting in my room studying when Jones came in.

"Let's go get stoned," he proposed.

"All right!" Mickey said loudly. He was from California and couldn't believe that neither Phil nor I had "got baked" before. Phil, for his part, nodded, then looked at me nervously.

If my friends were in, so was I. We put on jackets and hats — dark clothes — it was after check-in, so we had to play at being spies. From the very start, there was something extremely exciting about breaking the rules. The mere notion of it was more exhilarating than the inebriation we seemed to pursue with such nervous enthusiasm. But for Jones, of course, it was pursued with relaxation, calm, ease, and indifference.

"Time to get the newbs stoned," he said matter-of-factly. This casualness only made me more nervous. There must be something wrong with going out and smoking this drug. If Jones could be so sanguine about it, he was crazy. And I was following him. I didn't ask myself what that made me.

We headed across the bridge that led from our dorm to the hockey rink. He walked as if it were all an amusing game and not potentially the end of the world; as though he didn't even care if we got caught because the rules weren't really for him. They were for people like me, I thought, people who hadn't "grown up on pot."

The bridge to the hockey rink was new and sort of flimsy, with green railings over the series of ponds. I remember jumping off it in the spring later that year. It would be one more test of our masculinity. Everyone knew the rumor about a kid who jumped off the dam out in those woods where students went to smoke pot or trip on acid. According to legend, the kid had castrated himself on a branch that was hiding beneath the surface of the water, lodged in the mud at the bottom and sticking up. Like that unfortunate kid of our folklore, we couldn't see beneath the black surface into the silt and mud of the pond. But we jumped anyway. If our buddies did it, we had to. It was enough that they took the risk and survived; we had an obligation to them.

It was in the same spirit that night that I plunged from the bridge into the dark woods behind the hockey rink. I thought about getting caught. What would my parents say? My mother would disown me, she had said; and my father wouldn't be too pleased either. And then I would have to face the ogre-like administrators. What would they do to me? But none of us had time to talk about our worries.

Where two paths converged and led as one into a pine grove, we stopped. Saplings and bushes that grew up to our shoulders hid us from the flood lights on the outside of the rink. Jones took out a joint; we clutched at it with numb fingers, but the joint scorched them as it burned down to the end.

When we finished, the four of us started back to the dorm. I felt even more like a commando now than I had at first. With the marijuana in my mind, coursing through my body, distances lengthened. I became hilariously separated from the normal physical landscape. The ground seemed to give slightly beneath me with each step. An inner warmth replaced the cold I had felt.

As we crept back toward the dorm over the soft pine needles with the tall pines and floodlights overhead, I felt as though I was on a stage and watching a movie — a simultaneous sense of being watched and watching. As I slinked paranoiacally beneath the stark floodlights, events seemed to play themselves out before me; I was relaxed that they seemed separate from me and beyond my control. As we crossed the bridge again, I laughed out loud. The bridge felt elastic, as though it were a strange trampoline strung between the two banks. It fell back and bounced up with each step. Walking had become strange, even without the bridge. I wasn't quite there even though my awareness was heightened. The risk of getting caught, of getting in trouble, weighed on me. But, at the same time, it seemed irrelevant.

I'd never successfully smoked pot before. I had tried, but I never really liked it or the idea of smoking the stuff. In fact, it had always terrified me. A teacher back at home had once accused me of being a pot-head long before I'd even touched it. I told myself that I might as well find out what exactly I was being accused of, and had tried smoking dope the summer before I went to boarding school. That first time, I was still too scared to inhale fully, so it didn't work. This time it did. So, indeed, there was compliance on my part.

Of the two other newbs, only one was stoned, Micky from California who had done it before. He would leave school at Christmas vacation, go back to Marin County to devote himself to tennis; he ended up too drugged out to get anywhere with it. Phil didn't get high at all. He had just played at being wasted. I remember how he had tried to laugh with me and act silly. It seemed fun then, but the next day, Micky and I mercilessly ridiculed him for it. Somehow it was a sign of his unworldliness, his unmanliness, that he hadn't gotten stoned. After that, Phil soon got into the spirit of things. He eventually got kicked out a few weeks before graduation. He was one of the most brilliant people I have ever met. And in spite of his love of drugs, which increased and included a variety, he had an academic career that was in many ways successful. Even now, we occasionally communicate. He is a student at a small, well-known college in New England.

The night he got kicked out, he made the mistake of joining two students in a room that had been vacated by seniors, who had graduated before everyone else was subjected to final exams. One of the students was my roommate. His name was Mark, or at least that was what he liked to be called. The name, Mark, didn't actually appear anywhere on his birth certificate.

Mark was the son of an oil mogul, a self-made billionaire. By virtue of a trust fund and oil wells in his name, Mark himself had become a millionaire. He claimed he was a genius. He hated the Northeastern establishment, preppy people and their little high society. Strangely, he sought refuge from them by indulging in their favorite pastime, drugs.

I remember the drugs he kept locked in his suitcase under his bed: marijuana, cocaine, and toward the end of the year, hallucinogenic mushrooms, or 'shrooms as they are called. He took childish delight in his various pieces of paraphernalia. There were air ionizers, filters and water pipes, which, in conjunction with towels or other apparatus, could be used to mask marijuana smoke. As he put it: "The technology and methods we developed for partying were beyond anything any faculty member could comprehend or imagine." He had one small water pipe with a long stem to suck on and a cartridge for the water so it couldn't spill. He seemed to especially love using that thing or having other people use it. "Come on, just one bingo (puff of pot smoke) before you go to bed," he would exhort me. "It will help you get to sleep better."

When he ran out of pot, he would try such eccentric things as smoking freeze-dried coffee. It seemed that he would have even started smoking upholstery or "rug cheeze," if it had come to that. What mattered most was the notion and the appearance of flouting the rules.

That last night of our first year, Mark didn't have to resort to upholstery or even dried coffee. He had pot. He had never really gotten in trouble for doing drugs, but Phil had. So when the teacher nicknamed "VW Bust" came around the dorm — early in the morning, for no apparent reason other than to see who was breaking what rules — he was especially mad. He "busted" them all. "VW Bust's" epithet came from a combination of initials in his last name and the verb "to bust."

"To bust," of course, meant the same thing that "narks" do when they "bust" drug dealers. The word "nark" though had a different sense in boarding schools. It was used as a verb meaning to turn in a fellow student for drug use. I don't think anybody "narked" on Phil and Mark that night.

I suppose what happened was that "VW Bust" had heard noise coming from rooms he knew to be vacant; the rooms the seniors had left were next to his apartment. Sound traveled pretty easily from those rooms to "VW Bust's" door. I had been in another room, also adjacent to his apartment, where a bunch of older kids were fixing to drink a few beers and play a few hands of poker. Fortunately, I had the urge to go to the bathroom about thirty seconds before "VW Bust" showed up. "That was the luckiest piss I ever took," said one kid who'd left the room at the same time I did. He had already been elected vice president of the school, so it was doubly incumbent on him not to break any rules.

Phil had to stay the next day. Instead of leaving when his parents arrived, he had to have a talk with the headmaster. I remember him crying that night after the bust. He was so stoned, his laughs and sobs were almost indistinguishable.

Another part of the shrouded subculture was the development of intricate means of beating the rules without appearing to. With a high-tech approach to rule-breaking, there were seemingly unlimited possibilities for drinking as well as drugs, even though the legal drinking age in the state was twenty-one, and the oldest people at the school were eighteen. Often students who lived in town would have connections to people willing to buy liquor for them. Or they would make weekend trips on their own to Boston, or some other city, where package stores didn't seem to care how old you were as long as you weren't trying to rob them. Connections with school employees or cab drivers could also come in handy for buying booze. All you had to do was ask, and maybe throw in a little extra something for the buyer.

"If you had the balls and the ingenuity to get the stuff back into your room, then you had a liquor cabinet," Bill said. Bill's connection worked in the dish room, and would buy alcoholic supplies whenever he was asked as long as Bill followed the proper protocol.

By the time I was a junior, we had it set up so that you could walk into where you deposit your dishes after a meal and give him a nod, and that would mean the contact would go out to his car and leave his window open about a quarter of an inch. Later on, you'd slide an envelope into the window which contained a list of the items you wanted — and the money plus some extra for him. He'd leave the stuff at a predetermined time and place.

Bill and his cohorts would dress in black and position themselves along the route from the dorm to the pickup site. One would remain in the dorm room with an open trunk waiting. "That was really the best part . . . You'd go out there; you'd have your cap on; you'd look like a spy essentially." For Bill too, the idea of breaking rules was at least as exciting and enjoyable as the act itself.

Bill would put wool socks into a knapsack. At the pickup site, he slid bottles of vodka and rum into the socks, to keep things quiet. Along the way back to the dorm, lookouts positioned at key spots would signal with lighters: one flick, if a teacher was in the vicinity, two if all-clear. Once he made it back to his room, he would hand the knapsack to his cohort, who would stash the hooch as Bill changed his clothes. If, after fifteen minutes, no teacher had knocked, they would drink some beers in celebration.

Bill said he and his friends used their techniques and networks to engage in daily drinking and regular drug use. He remains a heavy drinker, but he said, he doesn't drink as much as he used to.

Faculty members had different ways of dealing with the problems, or of not dealing with them, as was more often the case. Some knew what went on but didn't want to get involved, or liked the kids too much to want to get them in trouble for breaking the rules. Some closed their minds to it, denied to themselves that anything was going on. At the helm of this wonderland school was a benevolent and bespectacled minister, a man who announced at a meeting of boarding headmasters that his school had no drug problem. He lived in ignorant bliss. His religion acted as an opiate, addling his brain so that he would not perceive the realities of boarding school life. When I saw him at my fifth reunion, he displayed his usual, cheery optimism. An alumnus can only wonder what he actually does when he hears of drug use, hazing, or any other unmentionable part of prep school.

Still other teachers acknowledged that drugs were a problem, that kids drank alcohol and did other nefarious things, but they were not aware of the magnitude of the problem. They were the ones who believed that "education" — presumably about the evils of drugs — was the best approach. Education doesn't get very far with cynical boarding school students who believe themselves to be smarter than their teachers, superior to all people, and generally invincible. Drug education would have blended in with all the other propaganda that boarding schools force-feed their students.

Sometimes, teachers and dorm masters could not act, even if they knew that their students smoked and drank, or even if they were informed of hazing incidents. Students intimidated them either by force of character or the threat of making them appear incompetent. Whether or not they were actually incompetent, it is impossible for teachers to adequately serve as live-in disciplinarians for a dorm full of children. On top of the demands of conducting classes, correcting tests, and reading papers, being a prison warden of sorts becomes impossible. Like most people, teachers would just as soon go to sleep at night.

At some boarding schools, this dilemma is presented as a virtue, and rightly. Students chosen for their maturity deserve freedom commensurate with their abilities. Freedom of the students becomes a source of institutional pride, a symbol of the high calibre of its students. Anyone intelligent and mature enough to be admitted to the school in the first place, the rationale goes, needs little supervision. The other part of the institutional pride rationale says that the school's supposedly rigorous standards will keep the student too busy to dabble in any illicit extracurriculars. Having freedom extends the honor principle of the classroom into the after-hours world of the dormitory.

For all its benefits, this convenient line of thought ignores the reality below the surface; it serves as a pacifier to teachers, administrators, and parents and in effect, aggravates what it ignores. It is all too possible, not to mention fashionable, for boarding school students to be excellent athletes, good students, and heavy drug users.

The idea was to create a certain type of student, qualified to attend a specific kind of college. Speeches were always addressed to students as "the leaders of tomorrow," as though not only the Ivy League college of our choosing would be served to us, but the world itself, with all its power and riches, shining with fat and grease like so much mystery meat on a platter in the dining hall.

You could call all of this positive re-enforcement, but you can also see the burden of pressure implicit in such propaganda. Anyone who has ever had any doubts might find it hard to believe. But then, if you were there, you were, by virtue of the fact, one of tomorrow's leaders-in-training. And, if you didn't quite feel like it, you might feel as though you had to escape. To escape from the system was to break the rules; and even the overachievers and goody-goodies ended up doing that at some point unless they wanted to make pariahs of themselves. "They'd be like nerds and not deal with it at all," one student from my school recalled five years after graduating. "But usually most people got worn down eventually and succumbed. The attitude was to break rules at any cost," he continued, "because it's even more fun to break the rules than it is to get stoned."

To teachers, students pretended they were better behaved than they actually were; to one another, they pretended to be more decadent. School became a contest to see who could appear most blase, most nonchalant, least interested. Ennui and cynicism were paramount virtues. Talk of college, of success, and academics was uncouth. But beneath all the pretense, kids at boarding school did strive. It was just that success seemed so far off that they had to hedge their bets by pretending they didn't care.

Behind the halcyon settings and lavish facilities, the outlaw culture governed everything — even how students set up and decorated their rooms. Decorations became a sacrosanct expression of the student's individuality.

India-print bedspreads, or tapestries, with their rich colors and ornate, exotic patterns, became *de rigueur* in the conformity to non-conformity. Not only did the tapestries look hip, they were also practical. People used the big cloths, not so much to cover their beds, but to mask unsightly cinder block walls or create false walls within their rooms, thus the name tapestries.

I remember buying tapestries for the first time — the first of many rites of passage into the subculture. You went down to a clothing boutique which was also a "head shop," selling all the most fashionable drug use utensils — virtual one-stop shopping for the aspirants to the prep culture. I bought a blue tapestry at that store with dark blue vine-like patterns swirling in a sea of turquoise which I hung and still own to this day.

Tapestries could transform one room into several rooms. Or, they could be festooned from wardrobes and plywood boards to create labyrinthine corridors called "delayed entrances." My school's administrators, known collectively as "the Second Floor," took their first tentative steps to outlaw tapestries by calling them "a fire hazard." Odd arrangements of furniture — wardrobes positioned in front of doorways and plywood boards oriented so as to create a barrier between the center of the room and the door — were also deemed hazardous. The issue was a sensitive one, and it was always presented under the mantle of fire safety; the alcohol and drug angles to the problem remained unnamed.

Students were addicted to liberty or to taking liberties even at their own peril. They would not give up the tapestries. Ultimately, "The Second Floor" decided that free-hanging tapestries were acceptable as long as they were treated with flame-retardant chemicals. According to rumor (and rumor was rampant in these small communities), the school itself offered the fireproofing services to anyone willing to surrender his tapestries to the school power plant. There, in the shadow of the only industrial smokestack on campus, the sacred "taps" were to be made safe. It seemed like a red herring, a holocaust carried out against helpless wall-hangings. This approach did not work very well. Short of taking a lighter from room to room and testing tapestries, there was no way of knowing whether a tapestry had, in fact, been made flame retardant.

Most dorm masters let the problem slide — as well they could, each being prince of his own fiefdom. Law enforcement practices always varied greatly from one dorm to another, depending on the disposition of the masters in charge. Some treated the discipline problem with benign neglect. Others, driven by a manic devotion to the letter of the law, delighted in "busting" students. Still others were too incompetent or thick to realize what was going on, or, if they did, to do anything about it.

It was in a dormitory overseen by incompetents that the tapestry issue finally caught flame. An enterprising group of students ignited a roman candle in a common room. The candle spewed fiery balls erratically as it was passed from one boy to the next. One of the balls shot through an open door and landed underneath a tapestry, which readily burned.

All other tapestries came down soon thereafter. "The Second Floor" would no longer tolerate fire hazards posed by furniture outlandishly arrayed. The real instigator was able to escape punishment by presenting a mendacious account, which was corroborated by another friend involved in the incident. The least guilty person was left responsible for thousands of dollars of damage and given the stiffest penalty.

At most boarding schools, all dorms have a "knock/enter" convention, which means the teacher knocks and then walks in. This practice created a need for delayed entrances in the first place. "If some guy's sucking a beer or smoking a bong," recalled a student who attended a boarding school near Boston, "you have very little time to put the items away." Delayed entrances could buy almost half a minute between knock and visual contact.

"In order to get into the room, the party area where the couches and stereo controls were, a teacher would have to go through this maze of tapestries at right angles to get around to where the students were sitting. By that time, you would have put everything away," he explained. "People could be smoking pot, and everyone in the room could be high and have just done a bong hit within the last thirty seconds, and if your engineering was good, there would be no evidence of it."

Teachers must have known that tapestries covered up more than unsightly walls. Some must have felt disoriented or intimidated whenever they had to enter a student's room. Upon opening the door, a teacher would see either the front or back of a large wardrobe too high to see over and about five feet wide. As the teacher turned toward the center of the room, he would face a succession of boards and other obstacles, maybe a desk and bookshelf, adorned with tapestries. This barrier could continue so that anyone who wanted to gain entrance to the center of the room would have to walk half its perimeter.

None of these images seems to confirm the idyllic, pastoral, and academic vision presented in boarding school catalogs, or even the surface appearance of the schools. Nor do the practices of boarding school students indicate that they have been inculcated with anything but a desire to beat the system. In our relativistic world, the only guilt is ineptitude.

To be sure, boarding school brought me three of the most enjoyable and stimulating years in my life. Five years later, I am only beginning to fathom what its effects have been. If only to justify my own past, I remain convinced that my school is one of the five best secondary schools in the United States, and that my experience there was invaluable.

A classmate convinced me to attend our fifth reunion. It came and went in the manner expected. It was hard to tell how much has changed. Students complained of tightening controls. But as I walked down the lane by the chapel, a group of four boys passed me, talking. "Now would be the perfect time to drop," one announced. Maybe they didn't expect me to understand their argot, maybe they didn't care if I did. But I knew the only thing you conspire to drop is acid.

As far as I can tell, things are more or less the same now, five years after my graduation. In today's students, I saw images of my own past, heard echoes of the same expressions we had used. I saw familiar attitudes and the same culture. It had all been handed down to them just as it had been to us. Indeed, it seemed that tapestries were once again legal.

2

Hazing

by George S. Gibson

My sophomore year, it all started as a scene fit for the preppy handbook. Dressed in my little Harris tweed and gray flannels, mom and dad drove me to the dorm of my new school in the station wagon. A well-mannered student greeted us at the dorm steps and helped us haul my prep school gear up to my new room. There was an "everyone-get-to-know-everyone" barbecue dinner for the new kids on the lawn, where the parents jockeyed for the attention of the house master, and the more aggressive students campaigned for that initial approval from their classmates. I was nervous, as I had been at the same school for most of my life and was accustomed to being the "old kid," but was also excited at the prospect of being so independent at fifteen years old. My parents made small talk with the house master, and he reassured them that everyone would get along fine, that these would be some of the best years of my life.

After the emptied wagon rolled away, the barbecue ended and the house master retired to his apartment for the night. I went to my room exhausted from being on display in front of people who I desperately wanted to accept me. At ten o'clock I had my sweaters folded in the closet, and I was just hooking up my speakers, preparing for the noise wars of dorm life, when a senior came in with a check-in list and yelled: "Hey flunky, do you got any food?" I had just learned what I was to be called by the upperclassmen for the rest of the year. I looked around daftly while the senior opened my drawers throwing my stuff aside looking for something edible. When he had satisfied himself that I had nothing, he barked: "What's your name flunky." I told him. He checked off my name and left. As he did, he dropped something that sounded like a little glass breaking. I called out to him, but he slammed the door shut. I suddenly found out what the little breaking glass was: hydrogen sulfide, H_2S, a stink bomb. The little room was quickly filled with a rapaciously nauseating smell of rotten eggs. I held my head out the window for the next half hour, too frightened to move, too timid to yell for help to people I didn't know. I had been given my first lesson in the significance of being a flunky.

In other schools, flunkies were called "newbs", "juniors," "preps," or simply "freshmen." Whatever the nomenclature, holding the title of flunky meant that you had no seniority, that you hadn't earned the respect of the upper classes, that you were on the lowest rung of the food chain. Most flunkies were freshmen. In my dorm, however, the youngest class was the sophomore class. Even though we weren't freshmen, the hazing tradition in our dorm was the strongest. The seniors had unquestioned power; the juniors weren't far behind, and they all had learned very exotic ways to make the life of the new kid less than pleasurable. Parents were always quickly fooled by the exhibition of politeness the upperclassmen put on for them, as when they greeted us the first day. The juniors and seniors would act the same way around teachers — beating on flunkies was never too harsh and always in good fun (the upperclassmen were mean, but they weren't stupid).

On the third night, the raid came. There was a tradition in my dorm where there would be a "flunky raid" during the first week of school, and subsequent weeks, as the upperclassmen saw fit. One night I woke up at about two o'clock feeling very tired but strangely uncomfortable. With my eyes still shut, I moved my hand down to my side and felt a pool of warm liquid. I sat up in bed groggy and soaking to find I had been the victim of a "silent raid." The juniors and seniors had taken a dirty wastepaper basket, filled it with soiled toilet paper, piss, and warm water and had quietly poured it into my bed. I jumped out of bed, standing cold, wet, and naked on the bare floor, slowly waking up. I was on a hall which was mostly juniors, and the vast majority of my flunky counterparts were on the floor above me, where screams and water balloons were hurled about the corridor in a mass frenzy of testosterone. The flunkies that weren't scared silly were caught up in the ecstasy of the ritual. They gained a special camaraderie of going to battle together, somewhat like a "flunky team." Late that night, they joined together to strategize about the brutal things they would do to next year's new class. I wasn't so lucky. There was no consolation in being humiliated alone. I stripped my bed, took my sheets and blankets to the laundry room, left my mattress out in the stairwell to dry, took a shower, put on some warm clothes, and fell asleep on the bare floor. In the morning, I talked to the house parents about it. They gave their sympathy but didn't want to take it upon themselves to confront the entire upper classes. My temper changed from scared to angry. But fighting back would be futile, and complaining to most of my fellow flunkies would be useless as well. I couldn't single out names and complain to the administration. I would be called a pussy or a loser, so I kept my mouth shut.

Flunky raids weren't the only form of hazing I experienced during my first semester at prep school. As a new kid in the dorm, I was expected, in healthy prep school tradition, to answer the phone, change the channel on the television at the command of upperclassmen, shovel the front steps when it snowed, and whatever else they could think up. Many a time after dinner, I would rush back to the T.V. room in order to get a good seat to watch M*A*S*H. As soon as the place would fill up, the phone would ring, and a senior would yell at me: "Yo, flunky, phone!" I would obediently answer, rush up stairs to find the recipient of the call, and run back into the T.V. room to find that the senior had requisitioned my seat. Hazing. I didn't even know what the word meant until I got to prep school — insecure older kids beating up on younger kids to make themselves feel powerful.

During the first few weeks, being treated like a nonhuman in the dorm was reflected in my self-concept in class, and I became self-conscious and shy. The good part about classes was that they were coed and hazing didn't impress the girls, so a general cease-fire occurred during the school hours. Also, during the day, I would usually only see one of my dormmates at a time, and the motive for an upperclassman to impress his peers by humiliating me was removed. Even though people during school were friendly, I still felt as though I didn't count and that nobody really cared if I were there or not. The beginning of school was a tiring experience. I spent so much energy worrying about making a good impression on the other kids and fearing that they didn't like me. The simple act of going to class or having lunch with people I didn't know, but whose friendship I craved, was exhausting. After classes, I would often pass out on my bed, miss dinner, and then do my homework until I fell asleep.

After the second flunky raid, I began witnessing more exotic hazing techniques. One of the more interesting was the "whirly"; it was the upperclassman's cure for everything. One afternoon some of the sophomores were playing hockey on the flunky corridor when two seniors happened to walk in. The "puck," a wad of hockey stick tape, flew up and hit one of the seniors on the leg just as he walked through the doorway. The seniors had just been handed their excuse to have some fun. They instantly identified the errant puck-hitting flunky — he was the one holding the hockey stick and looking as if he was about to have his balls lopped off — grabbed him, and dragged him into the bathroom. The two seniors held on to each of his legs, held him upside down over the toilet bowl, and lowered him slowly to the water. Just as his hair touched, one of the seniors flushed the toilet with his foot, and the flunky's hair spun round and round. This wasn't just an occasion for the seniors to enjoy, it was fun for a few of the flunkies too. Because the smaller flunkies were usually the victims of whirlies — it was difficult to hold a large flunky above a toilet — the larger nastier flunkies would watch the event with pleasure. I never had first-hand experience at being whirlied, but I noticed what it was like for the small, always-picked-on flunkies. They felt so helpless and so alone. It's one thing to be ridiculed by seniors, but it's another to have your own teammates join in to laugh at you when you're down.

Another favorite hazing technique usually reserved for flunky raids was "goober" throwing. Goobers were wet, usually dirty, but not soiled toilet paper, which were bunched up in a ball and thrown at someone. If your goober was on the dry side it would hurt more, but if it was on the wet side, it would stick to the walls, make a better "splat" and a better mess. One night, a friend of mine came back to the dorm in time for check-in. He ran upstairs in order to tell the house parent on duty that he was in before he was marked late. As he ran into the hall, he was met in the face by a nice, wet goober. Four juniors stood about ten yards down the hall, laughing and congratulating themselves on their aim. Because your attackers don't give a damn about you, and you can't hurt them, they just laugh harder if you protest. Like the whirly episode, these are moments of instant humiliation that you don't expect, so you don't know how to react except to stand there and take it. And that's painful.

My dorm overlooked the center of the campus, and the path that led to the dining hall was just below us. One fall afternoon, I was walking by a junior's room and saw a giant sling shot contraption which they called a "funnelator." A funnelator is a large plastic funnel which has a piece of rubber tubing attached to either side, (the rubber tubing is usually highly elastic Bunsen burner tubing from the chemistry lab) which is used in long range goober attacks. The two pieces of rubber tubing were then attached to the sides of an open window. If you took a goober and put it in the funnelator and then pulled back the funnel, you could send it about a hundred yards. As I walked by, I saw the juniors aiming their funnelator at a group of freshmen across the lawn. It was generally taboo to wail on other dorms' flunkies, but the juniors and seniors in my dorm made exceptions — they would wail on any flunkies. In this particular instance, no direct hits were scored, but the funnelator operators were soaking up the fun as if they were pleasure sponges.

Even when you were in a room with no seniors, it didn't mean you were free from their wrath. Late one Friday night in October, I was playing ping-pong in the dorm with some friends. We were having a good time and making a little noise when one of the seniors ran into the room, picked up the closest kid he could find by the shirt, and slammed him against the wall yelling into his face: "Will you guys shut the fuck up! I've got my fucking SAT's in the morning, and if I hear another sound, I'm gonna come back and beat the living shit out of you." He was usually one of the nicer seniors. We were instantly quiet. He left. The only thing good about this situation is that it happened to a group of us and not to one of us alone. Talking about what a raging jerk the senior was brought us a little closer together as a group of flunkies. My friends were a group of more passive sophomores. We agreed we would hold back on our ruthless outbursts when it became our chance to be the oppressors.

At my school, being a male senior meant that you could not only do whatever you wanted to your flunkies, but you also owned any property of theirs you saw fit. When the menu at the dining hall featured veal Parmesan (or in prep lingo, elephant scabs), curried stew (moose puke), or Swedish meat-balls (runny cow shit), the seniors in my dorm decided that food confiscation was to be a more active part of the hazing process. One night after trying to choke down a chicken breast that was raw on the inside, I trekked over to the local convenience store and bought a box of Ring Dings and some lemonade mix. I walked up the back stairs and rushed to my room to hide my food, but the seniors were on the prowl. Two of them walked into my room and demanded: "Do you got any food?" I stammered and hummed and hawed mumbling "No" under my breath, but they had seen me with my shopping bag, so it was no use. I gave them each a Ring Ding, and then they told me to go make them some lemonade. I did. When I came back, they drank it and left giggling and grinning. I noticed then that half of my Ring Dings were gone. It was a drag having my junk food confiscated, but it made me feel stupid that they thought they had fooled me. I knew right away what they had done, but couldn't do a thing to change it. That made me feel helpless and vulnerable. I take it for granted now that when I go home from work, I don't have to worry about being attacked or robbed by my co-workers. Back in school, worrying about being attacked or robbed by my schoolmates was a fact of life. This wasn't public school in the Bronx either.

Probably the nastiest form of hazing was a cruel nickname. This was most painful because it was the most personal. When someone was given a nick-name like "whirly," "geek," "douche bag," "gomer," or "the masturbator," it was really painful. Most everyone on campus would learn the nickname through the grapevine, so there was no hiding from the personal humiliation of having your peers think lowly of you. My nickname wasn't so bad, however, during school it was devastating because I viewed it as a depersonalization. When upperclassmen called me my nickname, I would try to ignore it. When friends would use it, I'd be furious. Today, surprisingly, I use it with pride. A lot of things about prep school weren't so bad when I look back on them; they were just amplified because I felt more vulnerable to humiliation at that age, an age when a kid's concept of self-worth is very fragile, and when at the same time, kids build themselves up by putting others down. The two go together like ammonia and chloride.

To the seniors, hazing didn't stop at direct physical or verbal abuse. Some of the seniors hazed to such an extent that they really believed flunkies weren't human, that they were just there for their amusement. If a flunky had something a senior wanted, the senior would take it, not giving a second thought about abusing the flunky's feelings. Once I was standing near the phone room and a senior walked in to make a call. He got out his little black book, found the number he was looking for, then dipped into his pocket for a dime. Just as he was about to make a call, the phone rang. He answered, listened to see who it was for, then hung up so he wouldn't have to go find that person and delay making his call. I never found out who the call was for, but I guessed it was for a flunky. There were several times when people said they had called me, and the person who answered had said I wasn't in when I was. When that happened, I began to develop a paranoia of things that probably didn't happen. I felt as though people were breaking into my room to take things. I had a jacket stolen from the laundry room, and after that, I was always imagining that some of my clothes were missing. We had mail delivered to our dorm and then spread out on a table. I was convinced that seniors were taking my letters and reading them, then throwing them away. Looking back, I doubt that that ever happened, but at the time, I felt as though people were out to get me.

During the second semester of sophomore year, two things happened. First, the situation with the upperclassmen eased. When we came back from Christmas break, we weren't as timid as we had been those first weeks of school and began to challenge the more ridiculous demands of our elders. One afternoon in January, I went to our semi-convenient convenience store and bought a box of cookies. Back in our room, I put them in my bottom drawer under my sweaters for safe hiding — cookies left visible would be noticed and devoured by passersby in a matter of minutes. About five minutes later, as I left for ski practice, a junior confronted me in the hall: "You got any food," he demanded. I let out a meek "No" and continued my walk down the hall. After I returned from practice, I looked in my drawer. Five cookies were missing. I walked to the junior's room, opened the door, and gave him an I-can't-believe-what-a-jerk-you-are look and said: "You stole my cookies." "Flunkie, don't lie" was his defense. I looked at him as if concentrating on making his head explode. "I don't care," I said and gave him a that's-a-totally-pathetic-excuse-for-stealing look. Judging from his expression, I think he realized how stupid it was to steal. I shook my head and left. That was the beginning of the breakdown in unquestioned upperclassmen power. Hazing slowed dramatically in the spring; I even became friends with many of the juniors. Despite my improved relations with the upperclassmen, the situation with my classmates worsened. At the start of school, you will remember, some flunkies had decided they wanted to get a head start at being dominant upperclassmen, so they decided to be nasty to the wimpier flunkies.

One of the most painful experiences I had my sophomore year was having a trick played on me, not by the upperclassmen, but by my peers. It was during the killer month of February, when everybody gets on everybody's nerves. We had a telephone room in my dorm about five feet square. The door to the room had a glass window in it. I was making a call when three of my classmates came by, opened the door, and threw in a stink bomb. They barricaded the door with the sofa from the common room. The room quickly filled up with a highly concentrated rotten egg smell. I was in a "Catch 22" situation. My "friends" wouldn't let me out, and I couldn't breathe. If I smashed the window, I would get them into trouble and would be considered a total loser.

If they didn't open the door, I felt I would be sick or pass out. I started hitting the window, gently at first, then much harder. It was a very thick window, but I was getting close to breaking it. The wood supporting the glass started to crack, but I was getting desperate. I was screaming and my eyes were tearing. My classmates eventually saw there was no humor anymore in what they were doing — or perhaps they thought they were going to get in trouble — and opened the door. I came out gasping for breath with a look that could kill. One of them said: "Geez, can't you take a joke?" I couldn't; I was betrayed by my own. I found out I wasn't even really part of my own group. That realization stung. What hurt my pride most was having to explain to the girl I had been talking to what had happened.

My next door flunky neighbor was the subject of more attacks than I was. For that reason, and because he was one of the few decent people on my hall, I was his friend. Many times he would be sitting in his room and some upperclassman would come by with a stink bomb or a firecracker and throw it in. He would come to me and say "Why?" and I would say "I don't know."

Once he was taking a shower and I was brushing my teeth. A jerk from our class came by with a dirty wastepaper basket and filled it with cold water. When it was full, he revealed his ingenious plan, which was to dump the bucket on my friend, and signaled that I should be quiet. I yelled for my neighbor to look out, so the jerk dumped the water on me and left. It strikes me that the purpose of these domination rites was to establish superiority over someone else. If you are sitting around the front steps one day comparing stories and you say: "I nailed Porky last night in the shower with a bucket of cold water," it shows you are in control of him because everyone knows he would never do it to you.

Even though most hazing attacks were on the nerds, some cool people broke down every once in a while from the feeling of having their "friends" turn against them. There was a German exchange student in my class who was handsome, well liked, and had a very pretty and popular girl friend. One night in February, a group of the kids in the dorm were joking around with him, making Kraut jokes and started ganging up against him and giving him grief. They were all out in the hall in front of his room, and he had nowhere to go to escape the verbal punishment. After awhile he cracked. He went to his room and pulled out his stiletto, which he often carried around, and screamed: "I'M GOING TO CUT YOU; I'M GOING TO CUT ALL OF YOU." He started flailing around at the group, crying, and they backed off immediately. They didn't run away but tried to help him, asking what was wrong and saying they meant no harm. They really didn't mean to get him so upset; he was, after all, a friend.

Hazing was the most extreme in my dorm. In other dorms, the flunkies would have to perform more standard duties than giving up their Ring Dings. In one dorm, a designated freshman was required to wake up every other member of the forty-person dorm each morning at the time the individual specified. In others, the freshmen would have to call out the score while seniors played ping-pong. In still others, the flunkies were generally ignored, but then again, the grass is always greener.

Other forms of hazing included a technique called the "aerial wedgie." A wedgie is when you reach down someone's pants from behind, grab his underpants, and pull up vigorously. Depending on the severity of the pull, the underpants might or might not be ripped off. An aerial wedgie is when someone grabs you by the underpants, picks you up and then hangs you from a hook by your underpants, leaving you in screams and humiliation. I've seen it happen; it's not pretty. The most common place of occurrence was the gym. The victims were almost always the small, non-jock types. To the jocks, who performed the task of picking out the wimps to be wedgied, it was a form of punishing them for not having the common sense to conform and be jocks like them.

I spent much of my time with day students or kids from other dorms who made me feel accepted. One night in February, I was talking about my dormmates with a friend. I told him I felt ostracized by the other boys because they were always doing things together, and I was never included. We determined that the reason was mainly because I didn't hang out with them. I was advised to join my dormmates after dinner and spend time with them. That evening, a group of fellow flunkies were hanging out in the common room of my dorm; I went to hang as well. As soon as I walked in, one of them looked at me and said: "What are you looking at DOUCHE BAG," and I kept walking, out the other door, up the back stairs, into my room, and had a good cry. I wasn't accepted socially by my classmates in my dorm until the end of my junior year when I gained a little more confidence. It was a long wait, but worthwhile.

In the spring of my sophomore year, when everyone got back from spring break — tanned, rested, and psyched for better weather ahead — people, even the seniors, were in better spirits and more friendly. We flunkies had paid most of our dues, and the seniors were too involved in their senior projects and getting mentally prepared for college to bother with us. After sophomore year, things improved gradually. As a junior, I was no longer the object of upperclassmen punishment. I had to deal with kids from my own class. After a while, when they got to know me, things went very well. Living on the same floor with my peers made a big difference.

Hazing was not just limited to my school. Friends of mine from other prep schools rattled off equally harsh tales. One prep school was very high-powered socially. Instead of excessive hazing, if you weren't "accepted" socially, you were ignored completely by those who were of the chosen social set. In some ways, hazing is a better fate because at least it is less personal, and people pay attention to you. Being ignored is a deeply personal feeling of rejection, especially in a partying school.

Throughout my prep school career, I would see people crack from hazing of one form or another, whether in my dorm, my school, or elsewhere. When I was a junior, one of the flunkies picked up a small axe one day and started threatening people. He was sent home. It was simply a response to getting grief from people. You feel threatened and helpless, and one day you crack and fight back any way you can.

One thing I always found puzzling was how little the school did to combat this problem. They noticed the obvious final breakdowns, but never paid much attention to constant assaults by the upperclassmen that led to these breakdowns. The faculty appeared to be like parents who had hundreds of adolescent kids, who never grew up from year to year, and they had given up trying a few years back — this is probably why school facilitates hazing so much. I almost don't blame them, but only almost. Faculty intervention could have been very useful. Most of the time teachers would honestly not know what was going on, but frequently they would look the other way, hoping that a colleague would play disciplinarian for them.

Remember earlier, when I said I planned to hold out on my ruthless outbursts when I became a senior and it was my turn to be a jerk? Well, I sort of lied. I occasionally made flunkies answer the phone and sporadically relinquish the slice of pizza, but I never "raided" anyone, and I never made anyone new feel unimportant. When I was a flunky, there were some seniors who treated me with decency. They were the types who had been abused the most themselves. I respected them. Looking back to my first year, there was one especially nice senior. I used to borrow his electric pencil sharpener. But one day, he was with another senior. I could tell they were talking about his lack of respect from the flunkies, (you could be liked or respected, but rarely both). I asked him if I could borrow it again, he shouted: "Hey jerk, those are my batteries!" He was instantly a tough guy, a little more feared, a little less liked, but a little more respected by his fellow seniors. Only when I was a senior myself could I empathize with that need. Once I succumbed to the urge to wrestle a flunky when he blatantly ignored an order. He fought back; I won. I felt the need to establish my superiority, not with useless punishment, but as a response to lack of respect. I didn't want to hurt anyone, but found I enjoyed being looked up to. It was one of the few periods in my life when I was the oldest — 6th grade, 8th grade and now 12th grade. I wanted to make the best of it.

Now, years later, when I see the same guys on the street or at parties who were seniors when I was a flunky, they treat me with the respect of a peer. They call me by my real name with an outstretched hand as if all is forgotten. To them, humiliating and torturing me eight years before had been just fun and games. Understanding that makes me feel somewhat better. I now realize they acted like jerks to be accepted by their peers, but it doesn't make up for all their behavior at school. I go back to school every once in awhile and hear from younger friends that the demeanor in my dorm has changed a little due to new stricter house parents, but the underlying hazing tradition is still there.

3

Growing Up Sexually

by Samantha Stephens

Although sexual relationships were not openly encouraged at boarding school, they were certainly prevalent. As the old saying goes: "Rules are made to be broken." Quite a number of ways to break the rules existed. Sexual intercourse was possible not only off campus, but on campus as well. Besides in the dorms, kids snuck into the chapel, the darkroom, or even into deserted stairwells.

At night, one could sneak into another dorm to be with someone by waiting until after eleven o'clock check-in, and then until everyone seemed to be asleep. Running across campus in the middle of the night was risky because of the campus security guard, but our dorms were close enough together that it took only a few minutes at most. There were ways, usually prearranged, to enter another dorm: an open window on the first floor or a fire escape door propped open. I remember once I left my second floor room, went down to the common room, and climbed out the window. A book kept the window from closing all the way. I ran past four houses. At the fifth, I went up the fire escape where I was met and let in. After a couple of hours, I ran back to my room. I was never caught. The excitement of it all made taking a risk worthwhile. I also knew of a friend who had a boyfriend who lived in the town. On one occasion, she had left the dorm at night by way of the fire escape, went to his house for a few hours, and got back in the dorm the same way.

If you did manage to get inside another dorm, you were home free as long as you were quiet. It would be dangerous to stay too long; it was best to leave before dawn. If you fell asleep, you could be stuck in the dorm until daylight when you were most likely to be caught trying to leave. If you did have that misfortune, it was possible to come up with an excuse. This happened to another friend of mine. She simply told the security guard she was very upset about some family problems and had gone for a run before breakfast to think things over. It worked.

Sex happened at times other than late at night. The dorm parents couldn't monitor the entire dorm every waking hour. Saturdays and Sundays, when the dorms were quiet, were especially good days for sneaking around, however, rules did exist about having the opposite sex in the bedrooms. For the most part they were adhered to as long as an authority figure was near the dorm, so we would frequently get together outside the dorm. Since our school was on a river, lots of couples took canoe rides away from campus and hid out in the woods along the bank to be romantic.

Weekends presented numerous opportunities. Students were allowed to drink alcohol at parties off campus as long as parental consent was given. To discourage drinking and driving, these parties became huge coed slumber parties. Realistically, boarders couldn't be expected to return to campus by curfew after being at a party. Sex occurred at these parties, especially if drinking was involved. Although not everyone did, many couples spent the night together. Going to bed before most of the other party-goers insured a nice comfortable secluded place to sleep. Other couples "made out" in parked cars by the house. Back on campus at brunch the next morning, we gossiped about who had gotten together the night before. Since everyone had permission to be at the party, what happened was up to the students there.

On weekends, a "sign out" system was set up in order for boarders to let the house parents know where they would be staying over night. Usually, but not always, dorm parents would call the house to check with the host parents that the student was actually there. It was fairly easy to get around this rule. One way was to "sign out" to a friend's house and have the friend cover for you. When the dorm parents called, the friend would be sure to answer the phone and say that the parents were out for dinner and wouldn't be back until late, but that everything was okay. After all, high school students don't need baby-sitters. With this taken care of, it was easy to stay at a boy/girlfriend's house whose parents were away. Once I came close to getting caught doing this. I had signed out to a friend's house and had actually gone to spend the weekend at a boyfriend's house whose parents were out of town. The dorm parent called my friend's house. He asked to speak to her parents, who, of course, were "not at home." He next asked to speak with me. My friend said I was in the shower and quickly called me at my boyfriend's house. I then called up the house parent. In the end, it was fine, but if the dorm parent had called back the friend's house, I would have been busted.

Another time, I signed out to a friend's house and instead spent the night in my boyfriend's room on campus. His roommate was gone for the weekend. I hid in the closet during "check-in" and casually walked out the next morning. I must give credit to a friend of mine, who was a senior at the time, for coming up with that plan. Other students were considered lucky because their parents didn't mind if they had overnight guests of the opposite sex. Some of the older students had lovers who had recently graduated and were at nearby colleges. Weekend visits were not restricted or chaperoned. One roommate of mine had a boyfriend who was much older than us at the time. They used to rent a room in a local motel when he came to visit. This was expensive, so it wasn't commonly done, but it did happen.

Basically, if you were clever enough, you could break the rules repeatedly and not get caught.

The use of birth control varied around campus. However archaic it may sound, the withdrawal method was still one of the most popular. I'm amazed when I think back to how many of my friends were having sexual relationships and using birth control sporadically, at best. I don't believe that those who were not using contraceptives were ignorant, they were simply caught up in the excitement of sex. Personally, months of taking chances and getting my period on schedule reinforced my behavior. Many girls honestly believed it would never happen to them (they could never get pregnant), and sex was worth the risk. Other couples perhaps had good intentions of using contraceptives, but sometimes just didn't bother. On the other hand, some couples did use them regularly. Birth control was available through a school doctor although this was not a well-publicized fact. The faculty and administration may not have wanted to appear to condone sexual relationships. I don't know for sure.

Having a relationship at boarding school was fabulous. It was very easy to develop an intense relationship, especially since you could see your boy/girlfriend at breakfast, lunch, dinner, and several times in between. In a sense you were living with the other person. The nature of these relationships, for the most part, was serious and long-term. Being away from home, away from one's parents, a boy/girlfriend could provide a great sense of security, comfort, and belonging. This was particularly true at this age when parent-adolescent relationships were strained. In some cases the parents were so far away, figuratively and literally, that they were unaware of relationships that developed. In the close-knit environment of the boarding school, intimate relationships seemed quite natural. After all, a sense of community and togetherness was encouraged. I can't say for certain how much the faculty actually knew about what was going on. Sexual relationships were not blatantly displayed. There was a feeling that sex was against the rules. If you wanted it, you had to hide it.

Early during my junior year, I began dating another boarding student. He was a senior at the time. It was great to have a boyfriend, someone to hang around with. The relationship became more serious, and eventually we began to have intercourse. Fortunately, his parents were out of town frequently on weekends. Since they lived nearby, the family's apartment was a comfortable retreat. Bending the rules, we managed to be together quite often without either of our parents' knowing. We were young and in love. Life was great! I felt I was handling a mature relationship in a responsible manner. In one respect, however, we were very irresponsible.

I was no dummy. I knew what birth control was, and I knew where and how to get it. I knew I should be using it. Unfortunately, it just simply wasn't on my mind. My boyfriend and I had several discussions on the subject. We would decide we shouldn't have sex anymore until we got some protection. But passion was more powerful than logic. We just never got around to using a reliable method on a regular basis. Our situation was not unique. We stayed together the entire year. He graduated in the spring.

We spent a lot of time together that summer. In late June, I found out I was pregnant. After months of taking chances, I was finally caught. Needless to say, I was devastated. I decided to have the baby. My boyfriend was going away to college, and regardless of good intentions he may have had, he was basically out of the picture.

I was faced with the decision of whether or not to return to school. Within a few months, my pregnancy would be apparent. My friends, my support system, my future was at school. I decided to return that fall and live in the dorm. Later that summer, my parents and I met with the headmaster to discuss my condition. Although shocked, and perhaps uncertain of what lay ahead, the administration and the Board of Trustees allowed me to return to school. I don't think they could actually have stopped me, but it was considered.

Everyone knows that teenage girls get pregnant and have babies, but as far as I know, it doesn't usually occur at reputable boarding schools. After a long summer, I returned in September to begin my senior year, three months pregnant, but not yet showing. Although only some of my friends knew, in a school of not many more than several hundred students, news travels fast. I decided to return to school because I couldn't imagine myself alone at home with a tutor, or in a home for unwed mothers, from September to February. I belonged at school. I was a good student, and I had a lot of friends there. I wasn't sure what was in store for me. To put it mildly, this was the beginning of a very difficult year.

As I mentioned before, at first not everyone knew I was pregnant. Baggy jeans hid the weight I was gaining. One day in the cafeteria, I remember a guy joking, saying: "That shirt really makes you look pregnant." He had no idea until I answered, "I am." It was a pretty embarrassing situation. As nature took its course, it wasn't long before the entire school knew. At first, I felt like everyone was walking on thin ice around me. Eventually, they got used to it. I think a lot of people had a very difficult time knowing what to say to me. Some tried to act like everything was the same, but it wasn't.

Being seventeen, a high school senior, and pregnant was not a lot of fun. Besides the physical pain, I think one of the things that made me suffer most was my inability to participate in many activities that were important to student life. During my first three years of high school, I was a great athlete. I loved playing field hockey and lacrosse. Being pregnant, varsity hockey that fall was out of the question. I missed being on the team. I watched them play and cheered them on at home games. It was heartbreaking knowing that I should have been out on the field with them. Certainly, my social life also suffered. No boy dared ask me out, and I couldn't blame them. I heard about parties, but was never invited. I probably wouldn't have gone anyway. At a time when peers were so important, I felt I didn't belong anymore. I would have given anything to be able to fit into a pair of jeans and go out on a Saturday night. Instead, I was wearing maternity dresses and practicing my breathing. I did have fun shopping, going to movies, etc., but I could no longer participate in a lot of typical boarding school fun. Since the father of the baby was far away, I felt very alone. Besides that, I felt fat and ugly. It was a nightmare. Nonetheless, I was glad to be at school.

I did consider going to a home for unwed mothers, but after visiting it, I knew I couldn't. I wanted to be with my friends. I wanted to take classes at my school, and most of all, I wanted the senior status that I had waited for so long. I tried to do everything as "normally as possible." At the time, I felt that by leaving school, I would have been copping out, running away and hiding. I was in a sheltered environment. Even the people who worked in the kitchen got to know me and made sure I was eating well enough "for two."

I was lucky to be in such a nurturing environment. Not once did I hear an insulting or derogatory remark. More than once, I was complimented on my courage in both direct and subtle ways. I had a group of very close friends. Although I'm sure that many people may have been uncomfortable around me, eventually I blended in. Both teachers and other students approached me and offered support. At times I welcomed it, and at other times I just wanted to forget it. At times I felt so alone, so distant, so depressed, that I just couldn't take it anymore. I felt as if my deepest, most intimate secrets were all out in public. But I was never completely alone, and I learned to deal with it.

In one sense, I was very lucky. There was one person I could not have survived without, my advisor. A woman with a child of her own, she was my backbone, available to me twenty-four hours a day. I spent many hours talking, crying, and just hanging out and relaxing in her apartment. From her I learned not only good exercises, ways to make the pregnancy more comfortable, but also how to stop worrying about everyone else and concentrate on taking care of myself. Her insight, patience, and caring held me together. We became very close. She took care of me and protected me. Without her support, I never would have made it. She stuck by me through it all. My friends tried very hard to be supportive, but I think they became frustrated at times. They didn't quite know what to do or say. I was a constant reminder of what could happen to them if they weren't careful.

Like every other senior, I was applying to colleges for the coming September. Because I was pregnant, I chose not to have interviews with any prospective schools. The seniors from my class went to the local public high school one Saturday to take the necessary standardized tests. I can't remember if it was the SAT's or the Achievements. Being pregnant, it was strenuous to sit and take these tests, any tests. Despite everything happening in my life, I managed to keep up my grades. I did miss some classes but not enough to put me significantly behind. I was accepted at three out of the five colleges I applied to and was determined to go.

As time went on, school became more and more difficult. I lived on the third floor of my dorm. It was tiring walking up two flights of stairs. I loved having friends nearby, but dorm life doesn't offer a great deal of privacy. I was embarrassed to be seen in the bathroom getting in and out of the shower. I wasn't much for staying up late and talking. For at least a month, I cried myself to sleep every night. One of my best friends lived in the room next door. I later learned she could hear me crying, but didn't know what to do or say. It was tough to get up in the morning and face school. Getting there by eight-thirty, after spending a sleepless night, was a strain. I was jealous of every other girl there. It was hard not to be depressed. Physically, I was uncomfortable. I felt scared, guilty, tense, angry, impatient, lonely, frustrated, and confused.

Classes at my prep school were small; I couldn't hide. Sometimes, I just didn't have the energy to pay attention. One day during class, I felt the baby kicking. I was very excited and very happy. A friend sitting next to me asked to feel it also. Although it was a happy moment, it was a pretty strange thing to be doing during math class. The fatter I got, the more uncomfortable it was to sit at those desks with the attached chairs. I could barely fit behind them. Somehow I managed to keep up with my work. My teachers didn't give me extra leeway in terms of assignments until close to the baby's due date. I respected them for treating me like everyone else. After all, I was in school to learn.

I delivered a baby boy in late February and returned to school in March. The baby was adopted five days after he was born. I loved him. After spending six months of my senior year at school pregnant, I was back. Everything was not exactly back to normal, but I was working on it. I talked a lot to students who had been adopted, and also faculty members who had adopted children of their own. I can never repay the love and support I was given by many. Although my experience was painful, it was a chance for me to learn a great deal about myself. I wouldn't wish it upon anyone, but it is possible to be pregnant, go to school, have a child, and still be able to go to college the next year. I am not advocating teen pregnancy. I am simply showing that when faced with one of the most challenging experiences of my life, I was able to successfully finish my senior year at prep school. No one was happier than I was at graduation.

I believe I touched the lives of many people that year as well as being touched by them. I did become distant from some friends and closer to others. I know my "situation" made some girls think twice before having unprotected sex. In a letter I received after giving a talk to the entire school about my experience, my advisor wrote: "Another milestone, another opportunity for us to confront your courageousness; another opportunity to simultaneously experience such deep sadness and great joy. You were beautiful, composed, and honest. I and many others feel it was an honor to have you speak to us . . . ."

I tried to think back and remember if any type of sex education, birth control, etc. was ever discussed. I could remember only one gathering that dealt with these issues. It was during my sophomore year. I do remember frequent attempts made by the faculty and administration to educate the students on the dangers of drug abuse. Our sex lives were not a hot topic at that time. I don't know if the faculty were simply unaware that sex occurred on campus, or if they chose not to deal with it. If as much emphasis is placed on contraceptive use as is on drug use among students, they would learn how important it is. Granted, for most teenagers, sex is still an embarrassing, but infinitely intriguing, topic. Candid advice about sexual relationships and contraceptives should be available. And, it should be available again and again and again. In a situation such as a boarding school, where many teenagers are together in a close, extended way, the faculty and administration have a responsibility to teach not only mathematics and English, but life's lessons as well. Maybe then, students would be more compelled to think realistically before engaging in sexual relationships.

4

That Confusing Wall of Color

by Moxie B. Benevolent

I came to prep school on a Sunday morning. It was my first trip to Massachusetts. I wasn't sure if I was ready to live away from home at fifteen — not just away, but three thousand miles away and in a very different environment. I had found out about boarding schools through "A Better Chance" (ABC). ABC is a talent search program usually found in larger cities. It introduces urban minorities to the idea of boarding school and offers boarding school admission officers the opportunity to broaden their institutions culturally. The beauty of New England in the fall combined with what appeared from the catalog to be a relaxed atmosphere of students and faculty made the place appealing. The image of uninhibited fun that boarding school movies had imprinted in my mind made me excited about the possibility of an unreal, fairy-tale life, and this excitement was what made me decide to go. I wanted adventure. I was young and willing to try anything.

My blackness was never so apparent as in this prep environment. I knew that being black had different meanings to different people, but what was most important was what it meant to me. For me, being black was not a way of life, but the way I saw the world. There are certain things that my color had made me see and understand at an early age that many white people had not had to confront either by chance or by choice. I felt comfortable being black and showing it in my own way. Unfortunately the school, Whites and other Blacks felt it necessary to define being black for me.

I entered boarding school knowing that the main factors that distinguished being black from being anything else were my sensitivity to other individuals and the fact that I would usually be treated differently than others. Many friends at home and ABC alumni had tried to prepare me for what I might encounter at a school like this. The warning that prevailed in my mind was that I might run into kids who had only had two kinds of contact with nonwhites: first from television, and second, as employees for their parents in various capacities, but none commanding respect. Upon arrival at the school, I chose to go in and be sensitive — that is, I wouldn't offend anyone maliciously. I decided to remember that I was black and that this had helped shape the way I thought. I would be open to questions, but I was not going to bring myself to the "White Man"* to explain why.

I felt a certain way. I was determined not to assimilate. What I wanted was the relationship I had had with the kids in my neighborhood as a child, but taken one step further. Not only did I want to "play" with the other kids just for the sake of having friends and enjoying myself, but I wanted us to bring an inquisitive sense of ourselves to the relationship so we could learn more about each other's cultural and regional differences.

Once my mother left and my advisor had dropped me off in my room, I was on my own. I was in my movie environment, my dream world. It was a combination of unbridled educational, cultural, and social enrichment. This was boarding school. I would make friends that I would be with not just during the school day, but twenty-four hours a day. This is what I had asked for, and this is what I got.

I had not been accepted at my school until a space was vacated opening day by a student who did not return from the previous year. Thus, by the time I arrived, school had started. It seemed as though everyone already had best friends. I thought there were no new students, although the few sophomores who had been there the year before let me know who was returning and who was new. I was greeted by arrogance. It was understandable; our age dictated that. There was nothing special about that in us, and there was nothing special about the fact that we all asked questions. The thing that distinguished boarding students from day school students was the source of our answers. Many of the questions we had about ourselves were never asked nor answered directly. The answers came from what other people did or said. As boarding students, we had to watch the actions of the adults and any student who seemed relatively mature to answer our questions about life. We took their words and actions as conclusions to the study of life. We did not need to know the specific circumstances, and we did not care about the differences between the circumstances of our mentors and ourselves. We lacked the daily discipline that would have put our morality in check. Many teachers talked to us as friends. We needed that, but we also needed to be told that we were wrong and human. We just needed answers immediately. We all seemed to be great students in the classroom, but impatient, arrogant students in life.

I was a black student on a predominantly white campus. At first, this meant nothing to me. I had been a black student on white campuses throughout my life, and this seemed like nothing new. In my first few weeks, however, I was

---

*The "White Man" does not refer to all white people. It refers to Whites who are ethnocentric, shallow, racist, and or ignorant (by choice) concerning other ethnic groups.

mainly introduced to minority faculty members, minority advisors, and other minority students. I was told there were minority student meetings and was encouraged to go. I went. They were offers of camaraderie for a young man who was homesick. I did need some place to begin, and it looked like a sufficient place to start. I noticed there were many minority students complaining about the way we were being integrated into the community by the white students. Many minorities sat at the same table in the cafeteria, and white kids felt as though we were separatists. After a while I wanted to sit there, laugh, and generally make a scene just to see if anyone would ever come over and, as a gesture of friendship, break through that confusing wall of color that separated us. I was tired of bringing body, soul, and explanation to a lazy White Man at his leisure.

I failed my "class" in high society friend-making in my first month. This was the first school where I was not able to get comfortable quickly. At some schools, I only had to show I could play sports and I was in. In other schools, I had to be arrogant; I didn't speak to anyone, just to show that I liked myself so much, and I was confident that others would flock to me. Last, but not least, it never hurt to know the score of the previous night's game (any sport) or a good joke. I had been the new kid at many a school, and I was ready. But, I was shocked to find at prep school that it was not the supportiveness of the group you chose to run with that spurred you on to your individual success, but your instinctive drive to be unique among the crowd that attracted friends to you. New kids joined a clique first at every other school I had attended. After they were acquainted with the opportunities and idiosyncrasies of the school, they would join teams or clubs with the support of friends. At my prep school, you had to establish yourself as a great student, athlete, musician, or actor/actress before you really made friends.

I was not ready to try and take on the world alone, so I stayed away from it. I found myself alone quite often. I joined the cross-country running team, although I had never run long distances before. I was horrible and could not finish the course during my first weeks of practice. I think no one from the team wanted to talk with me after a workout because they wanted to save me the embarrassment. But, over the years, it became quite an amusing subject.

Every Saturday I played basketball alone in the gym. A white student in my class was always there at the same time, and for the first month he asked me each week if I was from New York City. I would always laugh and say "wrong coast." I would further my explanation by saying I had never been to any part of New York. It was true that many black boarders were from New York, but not all, and the way I see it . . . especially not me. I needed a distinction, and my origin was it. His mistake could have been innocent forgetfulness; but for a lonely kid with no one, it was a violent theft of the only thing I had, my background. The view that too many Whites had of minorities was simplistic. They are either from New York or Boston, on scholarship, and not comparable students with everyone else. Some people thought the admissions standards were lowered for minorities. It all seemed too black or white for them. All of the minorities hung out with either all Whites or all minorities. Either you were a part of the minority students group, or you were a part of the mainstream. People felt you had to choose.

Many Whites argued that the minority students group was racist if it did not let everyone in. The hardest thing to explain after a close friend or I had been affected by racism was that we needed some place to go to speak our language. The reason why the group was largely black and Hispanic was because of the language we sometimes used. Some Asian students spoke their native tongue and could exclude the White Man when necessary. Blacks have had to bend the English language to say what they mean to each other such that they can be understood. Anyone who has been exposed to the language can easily pick it up. In this case, Hispanics, as well as some other individuals, understood and shared this language. Had the meetings been open, there would have been no place for a minority kid to go after being hurt by a racial slur, or just feeling left outside by white students. Regardless of being accidental or intentional, the slur hurt. Sometimes the kid wanted to say: "the White Man around here pisses me off." He neither wanted to stop while trying to vent his displeasure and explain, nor did he want to use the White Man's phrasing: "There are a certain few elements in our society that have caused me emotional pain. This reaction I have, albeit painful, is probably an overstatement of the case. Although the people who caused me this pain are white, I do not feel that the situation was motivated by race. If it was, I am completely assured that it was accidental, and my reaction unwarranted. We could therefore consider the matter closed. If, however, it was not incidental, a direct apology to me would settle the matter." Those words are not just words. They are a reflection of a learned social behavior. It is this behavior that has stifled many minority groups for years and this pain that students face virtually alone. Most white kids do not understand how far those words go back. And it is those Whites who have a casual indifference to events that we, as minorities just can not afford. It is easy for them to say: "Be quiet and things will work themselves out." What they do not know, or do not acknowledge is that it is their money and their skin color that takes care of them. It is their complacency with events, that of the middle class, that pads the rich and powerful from the true noise of the poor who desperately bang at their door.

Many people had high expectations of me at prep school. I, myself, expected to learn more about other people. I also wanted to try some things I had not tried before, like playing an instrument or getting involved in a play. I wanted to broaden myself while preparing for college, learning always to keep my options open. My mother wanted me to prepare for a challenging university. My advisor, who came to know me quite well, wanted me to push myself, to see how far I could go, and he wanted to help me explore the vast possibilities offered at my school. My friends wanted me to have everything and to enjoy it. However, it seemed as though the school wanted something different from me. The institution wanted me to be everything for everybody: to succeed in the classroom; win on the athletic fields; be a member of the student council; contribute to other groups on campus; be a leader in the minority students group; shine in the theatre; teach when faced with ignorance; beat the path for the diversity committee; give direction to the trustees; and lastly, to have school spirit. They wanted me to go through the grind every day. They scheduled your life from eight in the morning until nine at night, left you one hour of freedom, then held you captive inside your box (or dorm as they preferred) from ten at night until seven the next morning. Of course you could have had more than that one hour of free time, but only if you never had to eat, shower, go to the john, or shave, things that 95% of us were prone to do on a semi-regular basis. The sad part was that that hour was never a sacred hour to yourself. Something always came up.

I believe I learned and accomplished the most my junior year, that is, with the exception of Latin American history senior spring. I was elected co-head of the Minority Students Association for my junior year. Jones was my co-head. He was a very quiet and strong leader who kept everything together. I think anyone would work the job twice, if for no other reason, than to work with Jones. We grew a lot that year. We took a group that had been silent and created a group that not only supported campus minorities, but was also a strong voice pointing in the direction that the community needed to go. Part of the job included talking with many minority students and finding out how they felt. I wanted to know what made them happy or sad and to do my part to make school a more enjoyable experience for everyone. I heard a lot of sad stories and felt for these people; I could understand. I did not know myself if I was enjoying the experience.

By the end of my junior year, most everything I enjoyed crumbled somewhat. Opposing philosophies with the coach forced me to quit varsity basketball mid-season. This did not seem so bad though, because I had gotten a role in a play my sophomore spring and my junior fall. Thus, this gave me more time to pursue something I truly enjoyed, acting. I tried out for two or three plays that spring and didn't get a role in any. I was very confident about my abilities to perform in the theatre and felt I didn't get the parts because I didn't fit the roles. The parts were not black, or I was not white, whichever way you chose to view it. I then made a decision. I decided to get an independent study directing a play my senior year, a play that had at least one major role a minority should play. This was a great idea. I could get minorities a major role on stage, something foreign to us at the time, and I could guarantee that I would be doing major work in the theatre. This idea lasted until I inquired about an independent and was told I needed a co-director, and one of us needed to know something about lighting and sound. My second problem was that I wanted to direct a play with a major minority role, and other than *Othello* and *A Raisin in the Sun,* two plays to which I was not sure I could do full justice, I knew of no other plays with minorities in them. I found a solution. I decided to write my own play because I enjoyed writing. I finally got an independent study to write the play the first semester. I called upon the services of a guy who had quietly worked on every play at my school to full production. He made the play a shining success.

This was, unfortunately, the only thing I had to look forward to my senior year. I had been thinking, looking back on what I had accomplished as opposed to what I could have accomplished. I had wanted to create an atmosphere where everyone felt at home. I had wanted an atmosphere where people could easily become more knowledgeable about the things and cultures that were foreign to them, making my school a more sensitive and accepting community. Fitting in too often meant someone had to assimilate. I'm sure you can wager a good guess as to who had to assimilate more often. I did not want anyone to assimilate or feel as though more people would like to understand him if he did. I wanted people to recognize the beauty in two people with different upbringing coming together and sharing and celebrating the differences rather than ignoring them. I felt I did a lot for the Minority Students Association, but had not done enough with the group as a whole, and I had not gained as many Asian participants as I would have liked. Early on in my senior year, I resigned as co-head of the Minority Students Association and began a new group called "Shades of Gray." The group was open to anyone, and I hoped it would encourage taking a look at the different cultures at the school. It never really caught on, but is still in existence.

My senior year everything came to a head. I felt alone, and graduation was not soon enough. The first two lines of Shakespeare's Sonnet 29 best describe how I felt: "When, in disgrace with fortune and men's eyes, I all alone beweep my outcast state." I wanted out. Regular late night cocktails and walks with a friend seemed to take me out for the moment. My acceptance in late November to the school I knew I would attend did not make it any easier. Soon I tripped and fell. I got into some trouble and had to spend a few extra days at home during Christmas break. I returned with only one desire and that was to graduate in peace. Along the way, two minority friends of mine were expelled. They were guilty of their crimes, yet there was something in me that wanted to explain what drove them to it; or was it merely an act of indiscretion on their part. The importance of most minority crimes was not the crime itself, not the fact they were caught, but why they did what they did. From those I spoke with, the majority wanted some sort of escape from the school, or they were very unhappy with their state.

This leads to the most important question: what should the institution do? To answer this, I must ask if the problems of race and general rule-breaking are inherent to boarding schools, or do the problems stem from the school I attended, the faculty or just the kids? I'd have to say I feel only 10% of the problem was the kids themselves or our adolescence. Much of the problem is specific to boarding schools. Put kids together twenty-four hours a day week in, week out, and they will have problems. I'd say that the most common answer was to drink or do drugs. I would not say it was bad though, because everyone had a belief in tomorrow. Somehow everyone knew that tomorrow held a sunny pasture. We just had to deal with or forget the load of today. The other thing was that the daily bump and grind had to be finished first. That was the one thing that could not be avoided, and that is the saving grace for boarding schools.

Part of the problem also lies with the school establishment. They have to realize that kids fourteen, fifteen, and sixteen years old are still being raised. There can be no half-stepping, but my school does not just half-step, it sidesteps. You can't bring young minorities in and say: "Mix in; I'll see you at graduation in three years." They want you to cope with the way others react to your presence on campus on your own. There is not enough minority faculty support especially for Asians. In my three years at the school, there was never any Asian faculty member on campus to try to help understand the Asian kids. This is unacceptable. The school was also unfair to the white students, who did not understand or had never met Blacks, Hispanics or Asians. The school wanted them, too, to deal with something strange on their own in their spare time. I feel as though a school is not committed to diversity until it begins offering classes in the areas in which the students are putting their greatest energies. That way all students can gain a respect and understanding for all other cultures. The differences will then be appreciated, especially outside the classroom.

The institution seemed to treat the presence of minorities as "the right thing to do." It was as if they themselves never had a clear objective for diversity, nor did they have the slightest idea what they wanted it to accomplish. It was as if the administrators got together after bringing in the different minorities, wiped their brows and said: "Okay. We did our part; we got diversity. Now let's sit back and watch it do its thing." In my three years at boarding school, the administration could only muster up two phrases. The first was: "We are a very diverse community." They never realized that this meant very little to the community because they did not know what it meant themselves. The second phrase was: "The number of minorities in the faculty and administration is up 33% this year." This sounds fine, but the problem was that two is 33% of six, and it was only two added to a meager six to give us eight. Even the percent went down each year, but the most significant thing that they never commented on was that it seemed that we were losing 50% of our minority faculty each year. There were a lot of white teachers who would stay ten years, twenty years, but no minority teachers or administrators stayed for even five years. Every time I had a bad day, I asked myself why I should stay for three years, when adult minorities didn't want to stay three, four, or five years. It was as if their age and experience made them know something I did not.

I realize it will take time and money for these changes to take place, if they ever do. So, what do we do until then? I feel the burden of coping with the situation will rest, as it has in the past, with the students themselves. These individuals must seek out everything that is good in all the people surrounding them. When times get tough, look to the good in who or what you hate the most and praise that good. Ride the good of today — no matter how small — into tomorrow. In that new day, you must learn from what made you unhappy. It will be tough, and sometimes you will have to get away. It will help.

It's funny. Sometimes you don't understand things until months or years later. I understand much better now. I often ask myself if it was worth it. I had three years of confusion and pain, but nestled in between, someone had snuck in some good times while I wasn't looking. I have a life time of memories. Not all of them are good, but most are — perhaps by choice, but why not? I gained some friends I will have for life. We were so close; we depended on each other as family. I'm more mature for the experience, and I think I have a broader outlook on life. All in all, I'd say it was worth it.

5

Townies and Preppies
Part I — A Townie Perspective

by Christopher Rivers

Throughout my four years at the public high school, my friends and I referred to the students at the nearby private school as "prep fags." I am not sure who coined the phrase or why, as it was not a direct reference to sexual orientation. Despite the fact that I knew a few people from town who attended the private school, I would use the phrase when passing the campus or observing its students. It was a convenient derogatory label for our private school counterparts.

Up until the time of high school, my knowledge of the prep school was very limited. It was commonly believed that the students from the private elementary school would automatically end up there. All I really knew about the school was that it was located just outside the center of town, and that it sent its students streaming into the library on weekends for information.

The public high school was built on one of the old town landfills at the other end of town. The lot was cheap and the size accommodating. It was not nearly as glamorous or well kept as the extensive buildings and grounds of the prep school.

The public school students had no real way of knowing the character of the students at the private school. Thus, preconceived notions replaced actual knowledge. Assumptions and generalizations were formed and labels made to stick. Because the members of each school spent their time at their respective schools, the only interaction between the two groups occurred outside the classroom, and that was rare. One thing was for sure: they were attending an elite private school, paying much more for their education and living what seemed to us to be sheltered lives. In spite of our living in an affluent town, we felt we did not have enough, or at least, they seemed to have more.

We considered prep students to be weak both physically and mentally. Appearing in casual clothing, they neither commanded nor demanded a presence. Because most of them lived on campus, their dependence on one another was much greater than ours and, therefore, they were much closer. The fact that the prep school is a private school with a tightly knit environment contributed to its alienation from the public school community. I think we interpreted the relationships in the private school incorrectly. Prep school students seemed arrogant to us simply because they attended a private school; they seemed free and uncaring because they had few financial responsibilities.

In daily contact, too, relations between the two groups were strained. We felt the prep athletes had no right to use the town athletic fields. We referred to them as fags and regarded them as weaker due in part to number and strength. The tension between the schools was fierce. We had a preconceived notion we had to beat the preppies in order to establish dominance in the town. Though the private school did win a good deal of the time, we still perceived them as the weaker squad.

One experience in particular seems to exemplify our perception of the prep student. A public school friend of mine was close friends with a prep student from her summer community. Since she felt her friend and I possessed similar traits, our mutual friend matched us up. I called the girl on the phone, and we talked for an hour and a half. Our conversation was encouraging; we really seemed to hit it off. She sounded assertive yet respectful, intelligent and fun. The preconceived notion of her based on the phone conversation and the fact that she was going to attend an Ivy League School led me to believe that this was my perfect counterpart. At the end of the conversation we set up a dinner date.

I arrived at the school at the appointed time to pick her up. Dressed in a semi-formal outfit, I approached the gate to meet this new acquaintance. I noticed only one person there sitting with her head in her lap, dressed in a cowboy shirt, ripped jeans, and boots. Thinking this could not possibly be my date, I walked past onto the school grounds. She rose, came over to me, and introduced herself as my date. Her casual dress and carefree attitude seemed to signify more than a simple freedom of expression. Dress at the private school was more casual in general. Because most students lived on campus, their choice of clothing from day to day was not critiqued by parents. The choice was free; the style was free; the attitude was free.

Granted, she would not have been considered a "prep fag." But in the context of a first date, we seemed to have two totally different notions of appropriate dress and behavior which signified different "schools" of thought. We were cordial, but as the date went on, my biased perceptions of her schooling and daily life were reinforced by what she was telling me. She did not seem to be very concerned with the demands college would hold. It seemed as though she had received an abundance of attention at prep school, yet, instead of taking advantage of these opportunities, was going to relax and take in the future as it unfolded. At times during our date, I questioned if maybe I was the one who had conformed to a straight line of behavior and attitudes and could not approach a new view with an open mind. But I figured her "I'll-see-when-I-get-there" attitude was the private school outlook on higher education. As our conversation continued, we talked about our schools. I told her I felt a big public school was the place to go if you wanted to get a diverse view of the world, to really understand current issues, to be sophisticated. I felt that a smaller public school wasn't as good, but that a prep school was so isolated that one couldn't get an education that reflected any understanding of the real world. She disagreed. Her friends came from fifteen different countries and from all over the U.S. They talked about every current topic imaginable. She learned a great deal about the world. She felt that public school was not the cutting edge on "sophistication" either. Clearly, both of us had fixed ideas about the other, and although neither view was particularly accurate, it was what we lived by. The incongruence of our views made our first date our last.

The division between the students of the two campuses could be seen on any given weekend night in the downtown area or near the prep campus. Separate groups of students from each school would avoid one another, continually bickering amongst themselves about the negative aspects of the other group. Generally these comments would not be direct insults against individuals but broad statements and assumptions about the other's activities or plans. At times, there would be overlap between the two groups — friends that used to be in the public system who had switched to private. However, with few exceptions, most of the students of the two schools rarely saw the living quarters or experienced the day-to-day schedule of the other, and they rarely joined forces on a given night. The private school students were comfortable in their campus "bubble," and we, with no center to return to, agreed on a particular destination and went.

On a couple of occasions during the day when I encountered prep students downtown, either in a restaurant or waiting for the train, interaction between us remained merely cordial. If I was with friends and we saw a group of prep students, we would either generalize amongst ourselves or exchange cold comments. In high school, the most acceptable behavior seemed to be sticking within familiar groups rather than trying to integrate different kinds of people by initiating a conversation. When our group was alone, of course, various half-hearted suggestions would arise as to ways we should make an effort with the private school students, but we quickly lapsed back into comfortable behavior. Many times if we saw a "prep fag" crossing the street, we joked about hitting him or her with the car. Although there was no malicious intent, this gesture symbolized the interaction between the two groups.

During my junior year, a group of public school students attended a dance at the prep school. The dance featured a reggae group and took place in the cafeteria. After arriving and parking the car, our group headed to the dance, avoiding the people loitering outside. It seemed at the time that a large proportion of the prep students were smokers, but this, too, may be an exaggeration. Inside, the students displayed that carefree attitude, dancing devotedly to the music. While no physical incidents occurred between us, there was an ever prevalent air of animosity between those who belonged and those who did not. Since the group of public high students was following one of the members of the school around, what might have been a cold reception seemed to be much warmer. Still, they made us feel unwelcome, and we thought their behavior was slightly abnormal. We left soon after, as the dance seemed to be too far out of the mainstream of public school social life.

Public high school social life assumed a different character than its private counterpart. Many of our gatherings occurred at private homes in which the parents were not aware of the activity of their children. In this case, the town police became the chaperone-designates to quell any disturbances. Since the state school system fought vigorously to encourage students to remain part of it, there was no threat of expulsion for us. Our lives were more independent, but there seemed at times to be an absence of authority.

Public student perceptions of private school social life revealed quite a different scene. The presence of advisors in the halls seemed to indicate that the prep students were always being monitored, and that this shaped their behavior with and around elders. The students would reveal their individual attitudes only when they knew the adults were not watching. Though the public school students collected within their own cliques, the absence of adults on weekend evenings assisted in promoting the individual behaviors. These partisan perceptions influenced and promoted some of the tension felt at the dance. The differences in the standard social life of the two groups may have accounted for our quick departure from the joint dance.

Despite the apparent animosity between the two schools, attempts have been made to integrate the students at a more personal level. The most concerted efforts began in the arts and have progressed to the classroom. Currently, there is a program which brings together both groups on a regular basis for classes. The roots of these efforts began during the time of the tricentennial celebration of the founding of the town. During that year, our music department and the student government received invitations from the private school to initiate programs that would integrate students from the two schools. In the case of the music program, the aim was to celebrate the founding of the town. A proposal for limited integration of the student governments was made in order to help alleviate tensions and provide more interaction between the schools.

Since music has continued to be a unifying element not only among students, but in terms of relations in general, the collaboration was a great success. Our students who took part in the program enjoyed both singing and interacting with their private school counterparts and finding out more about their daily lives. The concept of the interschool student government, however, was met with cautious enthusiasm. While the initial plan was to allow the leaders of the schools to meet and discuss problems, the overall feeling was to wait and see what the ultimate goal of this new council would become. Eventually the program led to limited academic collaboration, but the idea for an allied student government fizzled out.

In music and academics, students of the two schools discovered their curriculum was similar. Even in terms of the out-of-school activities, the two sets shared some commonalities; both groups appeared to lack sufficient focused activities. Though recent efforts have been made to create a youth center where all kids in town can go, this has not successfully come to fruition. However, in small ways, the students of both schools have demonstrated that coexistence and cooperation are possible. Constant communication remains the key for breaking the partisan perception barrier and developing closer ties.

The relations between the private and public schools in our town appear to be improving. Once two isolated centers of learning, we are gradually coming together in the hope that the educational opportunities will continue to increase, and preconceived notions of behaviors and beliefs which overshadow developing relationships will change to mutual respect. We actually share more than we think, but insufficient association prevents the two groups from fully appreciating these similarities. Unfortunately, the general separation in social circumstances and isolationist policies block the interaction of the two groups. This divisiveness deprives students of learning about different environments and developing closer ties.

Part II — A Preppie Perspective

by Arthur Clarkson

A "zard" was anyone guilty of the crime of living and growing up in an uneventful New England town. To us the only distinguishing factor of the town where we went to school was our presence there. We coined the word "zard" in typical boarding school coolness and indolence, lopping the first syllable off the word "buzzard." And sometimes we used the word "buzzard" too, when we needed to make the comparison to the loping, foolish carrion feeder of the desert more explicit.

"Buzzards" rarely appeared on our campus, a wooded, neo-Gothic oasis on the edge of a town that could have been called Anytown, USA. The town was originally a mill town, I think, and its Main Street was flanked by the dowdy brick buildings of the industrial revolution. Interstate highways converged on the town, cutting off Main on either end.

At one end of Main, a state route led past a shopping mall and through a parade of restaurants replicated across the country: Pizza Hut, Burger King . . . That route rolled up hill into something called the Heights, where there was some kind of military base or nondescript state institution. We had to go up there to see movies unless we wanted to see them at the seedy old movie house on Main Street. That theatre never seemed open. Like the dowdy brick buildings all over town, it seemed dead and empty, haunting us with visions of a past we didn't want to understand.

The Heights was just as hollow. Nothing lay beyond the facades, the plastic signs and squat, phoney-brick buildings. For kids in the town, there was nothing behind the surface, nowhere to go. Somewhere between Main Street and our school was the local high school. We never saw it teeming with students, because at any time it could have been, we were in school ourselves. Any kids from the town who came to our school, of whom there were a few in each class, had to live in dorms the way the rest of us did. They quickly lost any link to the high school and took up the mannerisms of their new friends from places like New York, Chicago, and San Francisco. Their old friends became "buzzards."

Sometimes we saw the "buzzards" when we went downtown to eat or go to the movies. We saw them, with their lumberjack boots and their blue-jean jackets painted with apocalyptic figures, names like Twisted Sister and Ozzy Osborn. We thought we looked cool in our rumpled Oxford shirts and LL Bean shoes. We chewed tobacco and tried to stay out of the way of the "buzzards," not wanting to inspire their animosity. However dim-witted and slow-moving we believed buzzards to be, we also secretly suspected them capable of acts of unspeakable barbarism.

I was always scared of them, so tried to stay as far away as possible. Sometimes they would drive by the school and scream "prep fags" out their windows. Occasionally they would even throw trash or a bottle at us. I was always nervous walking along the street and frequently shielded my face slightly when a car passed at night. I felt they probably weren't malicious and were only try to scare me, but I wanted to be sure they wouldn't accidentally hit me with something. To me the concept of the "buzzard" meant a public high school kid who hung out at the train station or the pizza store and who didn't like me.

I remember one rather unpleasant incident involving the "zards." It happened one night when one of my friends and I went into town in search of food to relieve our hunger pangs. On this specific December evening, we should have been studying for our exams the following morning, but decided that hunger took precedence over memorizing chemistry formulas. We exited Cumberland Farms and were walking down the sidewalk in front of the town's railroad depot when we heard someone in a passing car yell "fuckers." We knew this person was addressing us because in our town when an obscenity is hollered from a passing vehicle, it more than likely is aimed at the nearby prep school student. We turned and instantly saw the insult emanated from the mouth of a townie in a new white Ford T-Bird. There were three of them in the car, and seeing this, I felt relieved because in the event that a physical confrontation should arise, the odds would be three against two and not the usual six on two or sometimes worse.

I guess this is why I gave the driver a curious glance in return for his remark. He turned his car into the adjacent parking lot. We kept on walking, hoping they would just turn around and drive away. Instead, they got out and approached us from behind. In fact, they forcefully ran between my friend and me in an attempt to knock us over, holding their arms in front of them much like a battering ram. I wasn't too happy with this turn of events, and I don't think my friend was either. He was one was the largest members of the senior class at 6'2" and 200 pounds, but these ruffians made him look of only average stature. It's amazing how much larger people are in person than in cars driving by. The "zards" began their shoving game, and I began my praying game. They insulted us, and we accepted their insults. When this didn't succeed in bringing us to blows, they began to try to anger us by tearing at our clothes, clutching my friend's camelhair overcoat and trying to tear off the collar. My friend noticed that in the pizza joint across the street, a primary hangout of the local talent as well as prep kids, there were two friends of ours dining in the shop's window. He looked at me and said as politely as possible: "Let's go; these guys must be looking for someone else." He then turned sharply across the busy street toward the restaurant. I was stuck there, being held by the collar by some townie. In fear, I pulled away as hard as I could and ran across the road, not caring about the traffic situation. Fortunately I was not hit in the process.

Upon entering the pizza joint, I let out a groan of relief, and my friend immediately spat out the situation, being careful to point out the three guys on the sidewalk waving us outside to fight. We decided to stay inside and wait for them to disperse, however, they didn't budge. In fact, their numbers grew as more of their friends came by to see what was happening. Soon three different "zards" came in the pizza shop to try to encourage us to exit. We weren't about to leave; one look at the gang of townies outside convinced us of that. The three sloths, who were actually at least eighteen years old, entered and sat in a booth across from us joking about the foul stench emanating from our direction. The manager, sensing their malicious intent told the thugs to either order something or exit the premises. To our luck, they ordered one sole portion of onion rings while they waited for us to leave.

Finally, they got impatient, and smearing an onion ring on my friend's head, they left. The manager asked what was going on, and we informed him of our troubles. He called the police, and two officers responded in about five minutes. The younger went outside to check for the townies, while the older stood accusing us of provoking the kids' anger, declaring that we had thrown a snowball at them, or so he had heard. Actually he had confused our incident with another which happened almost simultaneously back at one of the girls' dorms. I later found out that a car had passed some prep kids from which came the usual taunt, "prep fag." The students had retaliated by throwing a snowball at the car. This proved to be rather unwise as the car stopped, and the passengers got out and chased the students into a dorm and blasted the inside with snowballs. One kid got hit in the face, but little damage was done. Anyway, we finally finished with the policeman, who I'm sure knew half the kids involved.

By this time, our headmaster and another prominent member of the administration had arrived. They exchanged a few words with the police. Then we all left, walking back to school since it was only five minutes away. As we rounded the corner down the street, I noticed a large car parked on the side in the shadows. I had a feeling it was the same group of "buzzards" waiting to get us on our way home. I was correct. There were at least eight guys crammed into the car. I told our headmaster. He looked at me in a confident way and said: "If they try anything, we'll mess 'em up." We walked by and the townies sped off, frustrated that they couldn't ambush us because of the adults present. I didn't go back to town for the rest of that year.

I'm not surprised we had a bad relationship with the public high school students. We aggravated them when we could, and they terrorized us. Neither seemed to know much about the other, but the stereotypes handed down through the ages added excitement to campus life. Occasionally they were reinforced by a confrontational incident between the two groups. I asked one of my friends to describe how he felt about the public high school students. His response explains why the situation hasn't seemed to improve much over time:

"Zards!" he said, "They live to save up enough money to buy Camaros: used, brown or red, often with racing stripes, souped up, rear-end jacked up eight (maybe twelve) inches, bad-assed tires with fat, white lettering on the side. They drive around town, fast, impressing their girlfriends (who smoke). They drive around our campus without their girlfriends trying to establish their turf. 'Hey, do you go to the prep school?' They love driving up behind us when we are alone — power confrontations. They yell at us from their Camaros; we run away. They are psyched . . . we're not so tough, they think. They drive away. They eat pizza, try to grow mustaches, work on their Camaros. Not a lot to their lives, you know, 'zards'!"

6

Depression

by Frederick Connolly

The more time I spent at boarding school, the more involved I became in the school community. I left campus very little, spending my afternoons and evenings doing drama, photography, and sports. I took advantage of the excellent facilities surrounding me and got so caught up in my interests at school that the world outside began to fade away. I knew every nook and cranny of the campus, knew where people went to do drugs and have sex, knew the rounds the cop would make and the extent to which I could get around the rules. I was aware of these things because it was necessary for survival in a boarding community.

I think my situation was typical. My peers also became completely involved in their lives at school. The campus was our neighborhood; the dorms were our homes; friends and roommates were brothers and sisters, and the residence supervisors were our parents. There was such a wealth of opportunity afforded us by our environment, yet, ironically, the same characteristics which allowed our experience as students to be so complete, established the conditions for what I called a "Hotel California" syndrome: feeling helpless within a paradise. Since we had everything right there, we never needed to have contact with the outside world. Consequently we didn't have much interaction with anyone outside the prep environment. It seemed as if we were existing in a bubble.

Living with my friends, I was exposed to all their problems without a break. It was different from just going to school with them. I woke up with them and went to class with them. We spent our free time together, ate together, played sports together. In the evening we studied in groups, stayed up late, and slept together. Just as in prison, in a mental home, or in the military, we spent all our time interacting within a single reference frame. It was a total environment, and I interacted with the same group of people twenty-four hours a day. I was under constant scrutiny by those around me. It was evident because we continuously commented on each other's behavior. Privacy could only be found in certain bathrooms, in single dorm rooms, and sometimes late at night when everyone had gone to bed.

At the end of the academic day, most of the faculty disappeared, and the campus became the domain of the students. There simply weren't enough adults around to keep track of all of us. The lack of adult supervision and insufficient adult support established both a physical and psychological void, which presented an ideal setting for getting into trouble and feeling lonely and depressed.

There were several instances when I wish I had had an adult to talk something over with. One such time was when I was an underclassman. I admired one of the seniors in my French class. It was a lively class with a lot of laughter, so it seemed normal that he laughed a lot. Sometimes he laughed very hard about things that didn't seem all that funny, and the whole class would become hysterical. We were laughing at our own laughter. Late in the term, he stopped coming to class; he had left the school, apparently as the result of a nervous breakdown. I didn't know what that meant, and I still don't really know, but at the time I was very upset by it. Although we weren't aware of it, his laughter had been different from ours all along. Several years later, when I was a senior, I often wondered, as I laughed with my friends late at night, whether my laughter was the good kind or not.

Another instance involved a student who had a very intense experience with acid on the freshman class trip. He sat at the back of the bus on the way home and didn't speak or change his gaze during the entire five hour ride. We protected him from the view of the adults at the front of the bus. This was not an instance in which we could approach a faculty member because the student would have gotten kicked out. But I never got answers to the questions I had about his experience or how dangerous it was. Keeping knowledge like this inside me made me feel like I wasn't in a very healthy environment.

The same was true whenever I saw my friends go off into the woods to a place called "Eden" to drink or get stoned. Sometimes they went to the graveyard, the town fields, or the sewer pipe under a bridge north of campus. No matter where they went, I always wondered if they would be all right and why they were hurting their bodies by doing drugs. I had these questions all through boarding school. I don't know if I would have had them answered at home if I had gone to a day school, but perhaps I wouldn't have been exposed to as much and had to carry it around with me everywhere. It made me sad to see my peers so out of control. I wouldn't tell anyone because I didn't want to get them in trouble.

For most children the presence of adults, who have already gone through normal adolescent dilemmas, serves to ease the learning process. But at boarding school, it seemed that there were so few adults that their cushioning effect was negligible. The ratio of adult to child made it nearly impossible for each student to have an older confidant. Thus, we, the students, tried to fill that role for each other. Furthermore, the role given to the adults, as determined by the nature of their job, resulted in alienating us. We were afraid of sharing our issues since most of them involved breaking rules set by the school. I wanted to talk with someone about my friends' drinking and my own sadness which grew as I watched my peers poison themselves with drugs and exhaust themselves by staying up all night. But it didn't occur to me that I could do anything to change this behavior which had become "normal" within our student culture.

It seemed that safety and control were the primary concerns of our residence hall directors. They had to be; our parents had entrusted us to the school. Beyond doing their best to be sure that we were in on time, cleaned our rooms and the dorm, and turned out our lights by eleven, our dorm masters had little time to spend with us. Those who did go out of their way to create a happy environment for the residents became exhausted or crossed the line of appropriate behavior with students. In going beyond attending to the basic safety requirements, they had to give up their personal time and often their personal relationships.

I have always felt it must have been a strain for the teachers to stay at work twenty-four hours a day. The paradox of the situation is this: if they spent time with us, they lost perspective; if they took time for themselves, they never connected with the students who needed them so desperately. Their plight wasn't simply that of the normal burnt-out teacher, underpaid and under-appreciated, but that of a burnt-out teacher, who, like the students, was stuck in a static environment. Unlike teachers at a nonresidential school, they did not leave the location which wore so heavily on them. It was their home. They shared their "plight" with us.

Students and teachers alike spent days, nights, and entire weeks within the same reference frame with no significant break to enable them to put their situation in perspective. Teachers who lived in the dorm played the role of parent to twenty to seventy-five children. It is difficult enough to raise a family of one or two adolescents. At school, it was magnified ten times. They knew little about us when we arrived; unlike real parents, they didn't have any relationship with us yet. In most cases, no relationship ever evolved. We generally tried to stay out of their sight.

After I had been at boarding school a month, I began to feel somewhat depressed. There was never a time I did not hear about somebody's sadness. There was constant crisis, fatigue, and gossip. It was discouraging to be surrounded by peers saying: "I failed a test;" "I have so much work, I'll be up all night;" "So-and-so teacher is unreasonable;" "I got in a fight with my parents; my mom's a bitch;" "My parents are breaking up." We also talked about people we had crushes on or the awesome goal in the recent soccer game, but the dominant topics were downers. I saw my friends learn how to use drugs, then saw them "trip" to get away from facing their problems. I watched them change to be more like each other in their habits and their coping mechanisms. One of my friends had the following quotation on his door: "One should always be drunk . . . Not to feel the horrible burden of time weighing on your shoulders and bowing you to the earth, you should be drunk without respite."

I watched my friends get "abused" by boarding school because the school could not meet their individual needs the way parents might have. Prep school imposed many values on us. We needed support to distinguish between all the messages we received and to assimilate the ones which were appropriate for our development. It was difficult to evaluate them sensibly by ourselves in a basically negative environment.

The dorm scene was tough. There was a lot of teasing. My adolescent friends were not ones who tried to feature my strengths while accepting and working on my deficiencies to make me a better person. In short, we were kids, and we thought it was funny when someone looked like a fool or got "burned." Students tried to break the rules without letting the house parents find out. It was not the same as living at home because the consequences for unacceptable behavior were so extreme — you got suspended or expelled, and worst of all, your punishment was etched on your record forever. Liability concerns required that punishments be stringent. Because of the conditions in the dorms, we had a lot of issues we needed to talk about, but the fear of extreme consequences led us to turn to each other when we had a problem rather than turning to an adult who had the experience to help us cope with it. At home, it would have been hard to hide my feelings from my parents, but at school it was easy to experience a crisis without any adults knowing.

Our behavior and our language became more similar to the upperclassmen who had learned to survive in the culture. Our vocabulary consisted of extremes, and the tone of our conversations was ironic. This was especially true at meals and other large gatherings where we either tried to show that our situation was the most drastic of the group, or that we had come to grips with our predicament so it couldn't hurt us. If we expected the worst, then we could never be caught off guard by bad news. In more intimate situations, we talked to each other less sarcastically. We didn't need to put up our impenetrable facades since our closer friends were less likely to criticize us. Nonetheless, there was never a time when I could let down my defenses completely.

In time, I learned that the best way to avoid criticism was to act depressed. People were reluctant to cut me down when I already appeared to be sad. But when I was overtly happy, I was an easy target. A student once said to me when he saw me smiling in the hallway: "Sure you can be happy, don't you have any work to do?" So, like everyone else, I learned that I had better seem tired and overworked or else I wouldn't be "normal." I knew that we all had insecurities, but it was at times like this that I needed a home environment for a change of scene.

We started out the day with chapel several times a week. The speaker might be a member of the senior class and the topic was open. This provided an opportunity for seniors to talk to the entire school for fifteen minutes. It set the tone for the day. Half the time the monologue was tame or even upbeat. Many people talked about happy family memories, and some chose to show slides or play music. But frequently, the school or some aspect of it got blasted. Usually the critical remarks from the senior lacked substantiation. On other occasions, the school was spared, but a more personal account of suffering was handed down from the podium to the younger students. One girl talked about the devastating effects her father's addiction to cocaine had on her family; another talked about the shooting of her father. One boy paralleled the way the school failed to support its minority students to Naziism, but he neither substantiated his accusations nor recommended any solutions. I don't know if the seniors ever understood how much they impacted the younger kids, especially the new students, who were trying to get the scoop on their new environment.

The headmaster once said to me that teachers never know the extent to which they influence their students. He was accurate. We listened to every syllable of every word an adult tossed our way, even though it seemed we seldom paid attention. Therefore, the sarcasm and irony which frequently came from the teachers' mouths were devastating. These were the people who taught us, yet they seemed to feel as out of control as we did. The conversations I overheard at the teacher's table disgusted me. Topics bounced from bad weather to bad students to bad politics. Their comments included: "I don't know if I'm going to survive until vacation," and "The three best things about teaching are June, July, and August," or "Students will get away with as much as you let them." I guess it was their way of letting off steam, but these conversations reinforced their cynicism, and it would creep into a passing remark to one of us later on. Teacher talk at this table never focused on solutions; kind of strange, I always thought, since they were "teachers."

Teenagers, who are looking for causes to embrace, searching for meaning and a reason to live, can be soured by messages of despair from adults. I encountered one teacher who felt his job was to deal only with cognitive development. He felt emotional development did not belong near the classroom, and he told me so. In order to deter a "senior spring" letdown on the part of his students, he gave a short quiz on the reading at the beginning of each class. I fell behind and, determined to do the reading in the order of its progression, instead of jumping ahead to do well on quizzes, got five zeros in a row. He never said a word to me, but gave me back my zero each day. On the sixth consecutive day he gave a quiz, I turned the paper over and wrote an angry essay on the uselessness of spewing out memorized tidbits without synthesizing or exploring the text in depth. Not only was I intent on resolving this educational issue, but I was angry that he could be so far removed from the concept of student-centered learning. I was also scared, because I was failing English, a course I needed to graduate. The paper came back with a zero and a lengthy rebuttal accusing me of being an undisciplined student, who cared little about intellectual development.

The issue of whether or not I was "wrong" or inappropriate in my method was not relevant. We were both "wrong" not to communicate in a mutually respectful manner. This situation allowed me to realize two things: first, adult presence did not assure healthy dialogue aimed at developing the whole person; and second, I was feeling powerless in this environment — out of control. I sat through the rest of that class with tears rolling down my face, trying to hold in my hatred for him. That day in class is still my most salient memory of boarding school. I talked about it with a couple of my friends, but they didn't know what to say.

One afternoon on my way back from spring sports, I had the following encounter with a teacher on the street in front of my dorm: Teach: "Hi, how are you?" Me: "Great!" Teach: "Great? I'm suspicious." Me: "Just happy." Teach: "Hmmm . . . Must be The New Yorker in me." This kind of casual encounter, insignificant unto itself, contributed to the tone of the environment. Combined with all the other pieces, its negative impact was felt.

I had a wonderful relationship with a teacher whom I adored. It was one of my best relationships with an adult because I could talk openly about some of the issues on my mind. He took an interest in me. I was a better tennis player and I hit with him, so the relationship was somewhat symbiotic. Our friendship was important to my development and I am grateful. In fact, we are still in close contact, now on a much more equal level. He taught me to be very genuine and honest. He showed me that it is all right to be vulnerable when you are trying your hardest. However, he was also a tremendous cynic. Since I idolized him, I too began to become very cynical.

When it came to educational policy, he really seemed to have the answers. He called one aspect of prep school "the ongoing conspiracy." The basic idea was that schools get better by lowering their grades: they raise their standards artificially. The message: "Success is a function of low grades and a lot of confusing homework or, if you wish, 'pay now and pay later.'"

Although I did not know at the time, it was not appropriate for a thirty-five year old to portray such a grim picture of school to a sixteen year old. I idolized this teacher, and when he said "it's true," I believed him. True or false, his fatalistic view was a destructive attitude to unload on me. Different from prejudice and criticism, it attacked the central tenet upon which hope for a better future rested by reducing our environment to a place where we were powerless victims. The tone conveyed a sense of resignation to an awful and ironic situation. He suggested we were trapped with no power to effect change within our environment, since there was a master plan to which we were subject. I was desperately looking for an adult who could soothe my pain by telling me something good in contrast to what I was hearing from my friends, but the sadness was reinforced. It disillusioned me further, and, as a result, I gave in to depression. I became extremely bitter about the "hypocritical" environment I was "stuck" in. I hated authority, and I hated everything about the institution that was manipulating me.

I took the analogy further. To me "the ongoing conspiracy" meant the school not only deceived us through regulation of our standards, but through all other aspects of our lives as students. Lights-out and wake-up were set by the institution. These rules, which applied to everyone, were designed to provide regularity and structure. The problem arose when there was a discrepancy between a student's preferred mode of operation and the mode created by the school. So, it is understandable that in the case of students whose individual needs conflicted with the institution's normal operating schedule, the child was forced to change and thus feel out of control of his life. As a boarding student, I felt out of control because it was the institution that set every minute of my daily schedule. My friends' and my self-destructive behavior was our attempt to establish control over our existence — to beat the "ongoing conspiracy." The harder we rebelled, the more severe our consequences — punishments for not being at required school activities, loss of health, fatigue, sadness, and cynicism. We felt our environment had control of us rather than feeling we could impact our surroundings in a constructive way. Everything we did which showed we could have an effect was a destructive move. It hurt us and the others around us.

It seemed like I was living in a children's environment. Even the "grown-ups" acted like kids — they were as unstable as we were. It was a melting pot of cultures and a stew of issues all to be grappled with at an age where identity was uncertain and idealism was beginning to be rocked by experience. Essentially, nothing was certain.

The teachers were role models, yet we knew they were overextended: teaching, dorm-parenting, and sometimes coaching (the "triple threat"). It seemed as though they were as out of control as we were. We saw several marriages break up, a very normal happening, but one which is usually kept at home. At boarding school, faculty home life was as much a part of our day as math class, but much more interesting. The added strain a marriage breakup put on the dorm director carried over into the dorm. The house parent's sadness permeated our lives. If our residence master was preoccupied, we had to support him/her. This was not an appropriate burden for us to assume, and it reinforced the feeling that everyone in the community was out of control.

I was stuck in my rut; the teachers were also trapped, at least they said so. I wanted to quit school and leave this environment, but knew I couldn't without serious implications in terms of my college acceptances and others' perceptions of my psychological stability. Since boarding school was "prepping" me, I wanted desperately to show I could take it. I knew the environment was unhealthy, but I also knew I couldn't leave it without losing everything I had "suffered" so long to gain.

I wanted to escape, but felt the situation was out of control. The Eagles song, "Hotel California," became my boarding school theme song, and I sang it to myself inside my head as I walked around campus. When I heard it playing, I stopped what I was doing and listened. Eventually I gave in to the negativism that surrounded me. I became truly depressed, and I passed it on to the younger students. In retrospect, contributing and affirming negativism was not only self-defeating, it was a great disservice to my peers. At the end of my junior year, I wrote in one freshman girl's yearbook: "'Hotel California,' listen to the words." The song describes an elegant, mysterious hotel into which guests are enticed. Inside, they encounter erotic images: "mirrors on the ceiling and pink champagne on ice" and a woman who explains that "we are all just prisoners here of our own device." As the trapped guests try to escape, they must resign themselves to remain in their predicament. As the night watchman says: "Relax . . . we are programmed to receive, you can check out any time you like, but you can never leave." And that is how I felt as a student at prep school. My friends had their own songs. The Smiths and other pessimistic groups could be heard in the dorms. The scary part is that we all started to believe we had really found truth in the words of these songs.

By the time my senior year arrived, I had finally given in completely to the trap which consumed many of my peers and most of the residential faculty. I called the boarding school situation "the rut," and I described it to the younger students as an interwoven series of conveyor belts, each going in a different direction, and each one passing by the others but never touching. I explained that every member of the community sat on her/his own conveyor, being helplessly pulled through the boarding school experience. We couldn't get off because everyone else would keep going and leave us behind. The only answer was to give in or jump off forever. I believed I was right, and you can be sure that as a senior, I convinced several underclassmen that I knew what I was talking about.

I dealt with my depression by withdrawing more and more into myself. I was very intense during the day and very passionate about my cynicism. At night, I was a mess. I procrastinated during study hall and fooled around until it was time for "lights-out." I did some homework during this time, but I was easily distracted by my friends. Since lights-out was not enforced, we knew we could finish our homework late at night. I felt like I had so much work I could never get it done by eleven, so by thinking I had between eleven and eight the next morning, I would have plenty of time to do my work. That took a lot of the pressure off me. Besides, staying up late showed others I had a lot of work and could live on the edge with little or no sleep. Now I can see I had a strange mentality, but at the time it was very "normal" for all of us.

After studying between eleven and one or two in the morning, I would go down the hall to the bathroom with my toothbrush and washcloth, lock the door, turn off the light and masturbate. This ritual, which I did about four times a week, gave me a sense of control over my life at boarding school. It was my moment of privacy and my way to forget what was going on around me. It also helped fatigue me to such an extent that, although I was wired because I was worried about my academic work, I was so exhausted that all I wanted to do was sleep. I never derived much pleasure from "spanking" as we called it, but it was my addiction, my peace. I did not do any drugs; nor did I drink on campus. But I needed an escape like everyone else. When I was finished, I brushed my teeth and went back to the room. I don't think I ever washed my face; the washcloth was only a cover to explain the amount of time I spent out of the room.

Two weeks before graduation, I had become so angry because I had allowed myself to deteriorate to such an extent physically and psychologically that I begged my mother to let me quit school. Fatigue had taken over all of my remaining reason. I left the boarding department to commute from home for those last two weeks and made it through. No one knew about any of my struggle, and I probably didn't know about other peoples'. The faculty and my peers knew only that I was another prep school success on my way to live out my Ivy League early acceptance.

7

Covering For Each Other

by Lucy Emerson

My introduction to the rules and regulations of boarding school took place at my first dorm meeting. There we all sat, old and new students, in a circle around our house counselor, and one by one, we introduced ourselves and our particular likes and dislikes. Once we had gained a certain familiarity amongst ourselves, our house counselor proceeded to formalize the atmosphere and inform us of the dorm rules concerning the "evils" of drinking, drugs, and cruising. She told us the penalties we would face if any of us were caught violating the school laws, thus making the thought of stepping over one of these written boundaries enough to make one shudder. As I sat there listening and hanging off my new mentor's every word, I told myself that I, for one, would never jeopardize my graduation with such folly, and I suspect most of the other new students were equally intimidated.

Once the meeting was over, I began to wearily climb the stairs with my new roommate when one of the other girls came by and announced that there was to be another meeting in her room in ten minutes. We wondered what issues could possibly be left to discuss that had not already been covered at some point during the day. Ten minutes later we found ourselves and all the other new students encircling, not the house counselor this time, but the old students. It was at this informal gathering that we were instructed how to break every rule we had heard about in the previous meeting. The "evils" could be successfully achieved on campus completely unknown to our teachers and guardians. It was also not unheard of to get caught and still "live to tell" without getting suspended.

My mind began jostling first with the rules then how to break them. I was confused about which path to follow, but now the rules did not seem quite as threatening since they had been so successfully disobeyed. What stuck foremost in my mind that day was what the old students had said with all sincerity: the primary factor in successfully breaking the rules was watching over each other. The goal was not necessarily to save just your own skin but your friend's too. This was the first time I had heard the expression "covering for each other," and it would be something that I would later greatly understand and appreciate. A few months passed before I actually tried my hand at drinking on campus with my newfound friends. We usually achieved our inebriated state in my room. This could get rather nervewracking for me. I had learned that the key to not getting caught was your own self-control, control of your party, and plenty of breath fresheners.

I managed a narrow escape on one particular occasion when all was not in control. It was early on a Saturday evening, and one of my close friends and I were in our common room watching a predictable sitcom and wondering what to do for the rest of the evening. Three boys from the neighboring male dorm walked in. They sat down, and we began discussing what we could all do for the rest of this dreary night. My girl friend mentioned that she happened to have some marijuana in her room and would be happy to share it if we smoked in my room. I was apprehensive even though I knew how to stop the smoke from spreading into the hall, but I agreed. I did not realize then that one of the boys was already quite drunk, and the last thing he needed was to smoke pot.

Once in my room, I opened the windows and put towels by the bottom of the doors and hoped I could remember how to inhale. After passing the newly-rolled joint around the room a couple of times, my head was feeling light, and I began to feel uneasy as the smoke enhanced the stagnant air in my room. I decided we should go elsewhere and was cleaning up the evidence when I heard a thud in the now-open doorway. One of the boys, the one who had been drinking earlier, had fallen to the ground and was lying on his back vomiting over himself and my doorway. The other two boys ran to roll him over on his side so that at least he did not choke himself to death. My only thought was that if we did not get him out of the dorm, we would all be busted. With a little quick thinking and much haste, the two guys carried him, still vomiting, down the nearest stairs and out the side door. Luckily for them, they managed to escape from the scene of the crime.

Meanwhile, my girl friend and I were left with the mess. I only hoped my house counselor had not heard the commotion, as her apartment was under the stairs. In an almost delirious hurry, my friend and I ran into the bathroom and grabbed any towels we could find. We pushed the vomit into an awful pile and began to scoop it, towels and all, into a garbage bag. I then ran down the stairs clasping the garbage bag heavy with evidence, found a trash bin just outside the back door, and thrust the bag as far down into it as possible. Climbing the stairs again, I saw that the mess had been cleaned, but we were left with the horrible smell. I grabbed a bottle of perfume and tried, with some success, to disguise the aroma. Then we made a run for it, down the stairs and out the main door, and we did not stop until the dorm was out of sight. We finally sat down on the grass, completely high, not from the pot but from our own adrenalin after our narrow escape. We barely said a word to each other, but tried to catch our breath after our frantic experience, or shall I say, close call!

None of us, not even the boy who was sick, were caught that night. His friends had taken him into the woods behind my dorm and sobered him up to the level that his inebriated state could only be recognized in his conversation. When the time arrived to sign in, one friend distracted the house counselor, while the other apparently guided the sick friend to the security of his room and put him to bed, quite a normal occurrence among friends as I would later find out.

I was placed in a similar situation a few months later on my best friend's birthday. She had rented a room in a hotel downtown in which to hold a party in honor of the occasion. Some of the people invited had overnight excuses by false invitation. If the invite looked genuine, the house counselor generally accepted it without a call to the student's parents for verification. Hence, they signed out, hopefully safe under their disguise. Unfortunately, I was not one to attempt the fraud and was, therefore, unable to obtain an overnight excuse. We all set off on the Saturday, some of us until Sunday, and others until eleven-thirty sign-in.

The amount of alcohol for this party was incredible. It ranged from 100 proof vodka to rather innocuous beer and wine. It was all lined up on a bureau on one side of the room. We were having a great time as people kept arriving, and the room began to resemble a mob drowned in music playing from a portable jam box. A close friend of mine decided she would drink vodka and began to consume it in great quantities. I did not really notice since I too was quite happy drinking my gin and tonics, which by this time of the year, after many similar parties, I had taken quite a liking to. At about ten o'clock, she started feeling sick and did not leave the bathroom for half an hour only to return to be sick again. We all became concerned since she, like myself, had to be back at school that night. Several of us took turns watching over her. After much deliberation, we decided she could never make it back to school on public transportation in her present state as there was no way to stop the bus periodically for her to be sick. I, on the other hand, was far more concerned with getting her past her house counselor at eleven-thirty sign-in.

Despite the fact that I too was feeling ill watching her get repeatedly sick, another friend and I took it upon ourselves to help her back to her dorm without getting caught. However, I was not sure how well we could cover her drunken state, and if she did get caught, I knew since we were helping her we would be questioned just as intensely. In spite of our fears, we realized that without our help she would definitely be busted. I knew I couldn't just stand by and let that happen to a friend. We were able to locate transportation in the form of an older brother who was going to college in the area and was lucky enough, for our sake, to have a car at his disposal. We placed our friend in the front seat clutching the door handle in case she felt the urge to be sick again. My friend and I got into the back, silently praying she might develop some control or sobriety during the forty-five minute drive back to school. We all remained silent as we drove along. My head began to spin as I tried to focus on the rear lights of the car in front. A feeling of nausea developed inside me, but my anxiety over our present predicament seemed to overcome it. My friend just sat in front desperately worrying, she later told me, about sign-in and at the same time trying to pull herself together.

We finally reached campus, and with butterflies in my stomach, I helped her out of the car. As we entered the dorm, my plan was to appear to be telling her something important. I was to have my arm around her, really for stability, but to make it look like it was to pull her closer to tell her something confidential. As we entered the dorm, the house counselor questioned why I was not at my own dorm, but sounding upset, I declared I just had to speak to my friend for a moment. She allowed me to walk with her to her room. Once we were there, I made her get into bed and insisted she stay in her room. Her house counselor had fallen for the cover, so I didn't worry about her checking up on my friend. I made sure there was a sizable trash can next to her bed in case she felt the urge again and told her next door neighbor, a mutual friend, of her predicament. Then, very relieved, I hastily left by the side door and ran breathlessly to my own dorm. Afraid of the toxic aroma I was probably exhaling, I avoided my house counselor and hurried up the stairs to my room. I fell onto my bed and slowly relaxed realizing that I had just successfully covered for myself and my friend.

Despite that particularly close call, having a party off campus was by far the safest way to attain the inebriated state and always assured never getting caught consuming the drug of your choice. Unfortunately, most parties were held on campus for lack of a better location. The usual place was a room, specifically a double due to the need for space. As I mentioned before, mine was the common selection, but not all the time by any means. When my room was chosen, however, I tried to keep track of where in the dorm my house counselor was likely to be. In spite of extreme caution, keeping an ear to the ground for these "sly" beings was not as easy as one might think. The word "sly" comes to mind because they have a habit of knocking on one's door at the most inopportune moments to ask rather mundane questions. On one occasion, my friends and I certainly hadn't been careful enough.

The weekend my little sister was to visit me came around, and I really wanted to show her how much fun a Friday night on campus could be despite popular belief to the contrary. It was the same weekend that my good friend's little brother was also coming for a visit. We decided to have a rather small get-together in her room with about ten of our closest friends. The drinks provided were to be a bottle of Bacardi rum and another of gin, both easily disguised in orange juice or coke, the prized mixers obtainable from the drink machines in the dorms. We had acquired this alcohol from an expedition earlier in the year to a college in Boston where friends, who had graduated a year or so before, managed to buy it for us. On these occasions we would certainly stock up for our closet drinking cabinets.

Anyway, Friday arrived and my sister and I made our way through the icy winter air across campus to my friend's dorm. We entered her room to find everyone lounging around. After the introductions, we decided to bring out the beverages from the back drawer of her bureau. We did not worry too much about getting caught as the dorm was one of the oldest on campus, and the floorboards creaked terribly when walked on. Hence tracing the whereabouts of a slow-paced house counselor was not that difficult. Out came the glasses, and we all settled down for drinks and some fun. I had acquired a new boyfriend that month and was happy to sit between him and my little sister. After a while, we were all very relaxed and unaware of the increasing volume of our voices. I decided to make myself another drink and walked over to the bureau and pulled out the bottle of gin. Placing it on top, I was just starting across the room to get some orange juice when there was a knock on the door. Before any of us could ask who it was, my friend's brother had unwittingly opened it. There stood an inquisitive house counselor. At that instant, I was still close enough to the gin, and my boyfriend was on the other side of it and somewhat next to me. I quickly leaned over, and placing my arm on my boyfriend, pushed the gin between us barely out of sight. Pretending to be uninterested in what the house counselor had to say, I tried to casually glance over my shoulder. She asked a mediocre question about the date or some such thing and looked around with a keen eye. I stood there pretending to be cutesie with my boyfriend, but was really shaking and praying she would not see the bottle I could feel pressed against me. Somewhat satisfied with her brief search, to all our relief, she left. I eased back and hastily hid the gin in the drawer again. If my friend's brother had not opened the door, we would have had a few more seconds to conceal everything. Luckily, one of the girls who lived in the dorm had instantly walked up to the house counselor and asked what she wanted, hence blocking her view for a few precious moments. We had not been able to hear the creaking floor because of our careless noise. We had, however, successfully covered for each other as a sort of team. We had thought on our feet and concealed the glasses and bottles by pushing them under the beds or behind books or shielding them with our bodies.

Drinking at parties was not the only time one consumed. When a school function reached a new level of boredom, we felt it necessary as well. To spice up such events, we would drink beforehand or during a break — a common occurrence at my boarding school. One such time was when a friend and I were watching the school play, *Guys and Dolls.* The play droned on, and we both came up with a great idea to lighten the tiresome ordeal we were obliged to sit through. As soon as the curtain dropped for intermission, we clambered out of our seats through the crowd and ran to my dorm just down the hill. Once in my room, we locked the door, and I pulled out the bottle of vodka from the back of my closet. We both took rather painful swigs. When we had had our fill, I replaced the bottle, and we ran back up the hill more than ready for the second act of the play. We made it back to our seats being careful to avoid wandering faculty by stopping occasionally and ducking into the crowd in the entry hall of the theatre.

Finally, we arrived at the last act, and I was still slightly dizzy from our activities at intermission. As soon as the play ended, and we felt we had paid our dues, we set off for my room again to repeat our act before we went to the dance an hour later. This time I did not drink quite as much, but my friend was not as cautious. After half an hour of taking swigs, she wanted to set off for the dance. By this time, my boyfriend had arrived, and we both tried to encourage her to stay a while and sober up. She refused and headed out the door and down the stairs. We caught up with her, and I feared for what she would do; she seemed to be completely unreasonable. We placed her between us and walked slowly across campus to the auditorium. She began to put more and more weight on the two of us. I was still buzzed from the vodka and had great difficulty holding up half of her and myself as well. We gradually walked slower and slower, both my boyfriend and I gently trying to talk some sense into her. There was no way either of us would let her go into the dance in that condition. We knew if she did, the chance that a faculty member would catch sight of her would be very good. We couldn't just let her get caught since she was our mutual friend and would come to our rescue if the situation were reversed. We finally reached the auditorium and stood motionless outside the huge building, which for her tonight could mean being busted. At that moment she made an excellent decision — not to go inside, probably because she had started to feel nauseous. We turned around and walked her to her dorm. Once there, I took her to her room and put her into bed. Luckily the house counselor was not around, and she had signed in early enough that no questions would be asked. We told another student in the dorm about her state, just to be cautious. The next day, even though she wasn't eating, she came to breakfast and headed straight for our table and said plainly and in all sincerity: "Thank you. I definitely owe you both one!"

Keeping my friends and myself out of trouble often placed me in hair-raising situations. Drinking and drugs were not the only causes for such predicaments. I had a spine-curdling experience cruising across campus late one night. I had permission to sleep over in a friends's dorm and was getting ready for bed when my boyfriend called from his respective dorm, a considerable distance from where I was. He suggested I come and spend the night, which at first seemed ridiculous. I had never cruised before, and it was May, and as a senior, if I got into trouble now, I was liable to get kicked out of school. After much deliberation, I decided to do it for the sole reason that one of his friends, who was a master in the art of cruising, would come and escort me to their dorm.

We agreed to meet outside my dorm at one o'clock in the morning. I asked my friends to cover in case someone was looking for me. They were to declare me asleep or in the shower. Then they could call my boyfriend and forewarn him of any approaching danger. I carefully made my way down the stairs and out the front door. As my eyes got accustomed to the dark, I searched around waiting to hear or see my friend. Soon a faint but familiar voice called from a nearby shrub, and he appeared out of the shadows. He made me take off my shoes so as to make no noise, and we headed off up the street staying behind the trees. Everything seemed to be going well, and I wondered why I had been so paranoid earlier. We were about half way there, walking down a street of small dorms, when I saw a light go on in a doorway. I instantly froze as I watched a figure come into view. I could hear my heart pounding and envisioned the end of my high school career. My friend, in a much more composed state, whispered to me that we should walk. I was barely able to move, so he grabbed my hand and we walked. We were across the street from the dorm and slightly in the shadows. I was sure the person was watching us. We were passing in his direct line of vision, but he did not make any move toward us. Once around the corner, we ran along the back of a house at full speed. I was being dragged along by my friend and noticed we were taking a short cut through the graveyard. I stepped swiftly with my bare feet dodging the graves. Finally, we arrived, and I was slipped into the safety of my boyfriend's room. I fell onto the bed in an utterly breathless state. I vowed I would never, ever cruise again; that was just a little too close for comfort. My accomplice in crime did not appear to be too fazed, as he gaily added to the juicy parts of the story when relating it to my boyfriend. However, I must admit that without him pulling me along, I probably would have still been there frozen to the spot.

I graduated with a clean slate in June. I had gained valuable knowledge in boarding school, and a great deal of that was about friendships. Covering for each other is what friends do; they look out for and protect each other in dire situations. At my school, this was a mutual understanding I shared with my friends. Students tend to bond together to make life a little bit more exciting at boarding school. The faculty does not become the "bad guy," so to speak, but the law enforcer within the boarding school world. Hence, covering for each other is a necessary requirement to survive in that world.

8

Lost Illusions

by Cooper Sullivan

My first brush with my future prep school came when I was eight years old. In an effort to steer me in the "right direction" toward a life of success, I was required to accompany my stepfather to a function at his preparatory alma mater — a sprawling, baronial estate of a place safely tucked away in the woods of New England. I remember little of the trip except that it was dreadfully cold and seemingly dark all the time. The campus, featuring a uniform style of architecture which can only be described as English Country Home, seemed to loom over me like a foreboding shadow lurking in one's closet. As we drove away, I couldn't help but feel I had escaped from prison and been given a second chance at freedom by the authorities.

However, though my active imagination in those early years tended to link the idea of boarding school with bread and water ("Please sir, may I have some more?"), from my stepfather's point of view the trip had proven to be a success. A seed had been planted, and as I grew to appreciate the fact that where I was from the road to Stanford did not pass through our local high school, I wanted to attend my prep school very badly indeed. Gone were the Oliver Twist associations. Now, as I sojourned out on the All New England Prep School Tour, my future school, with its impeccable college placement record, endless expanses of lawn, and a bevy of beautiful girls, became an obsession for me. It was to go there or forever live in shame.

Thankfully, the shame never came — only an acceptance letter. Thus, starting from that day, I was unable to focus on anything but arriving at my new school. Having very little to go on but the catalog (not trusting my stepfather's archaic recollections) hampered my ability to create an image of my future home. So I allowed my imagination to fill in the dark patches with glorious technicolor fantasies of me fitting in effortlessly with the older kids, me starring in the spring play, me falling in love, me vaulting over the supposedly strenuous academic hurdles into the college of my choice. My delusions were

73

natural for an over-achieving fourteen-year-old confronted with an opportunity to be The Best amidst the cream (I was told) of the American crop.

They were reinforced when, not long after I got into the school, a friend
invited me there for a weekend to scope out the joint. I was dazzled. The campus, in the light of spring, was startling in its size and opulence. Few college
campuses could compare with the facilities we were provided with to study,
eat, sleep, and exercise.

I attended classes with my friend and was struck by the fact that in many
of the classrooms, the central piece of furniture was a large wooden table
around which bright and charming teenagers glibly or, in some instances,
seriously delivered their thoughts about Lady MacBeth or the War of the
Roses. The instructors, whether young or old, were attentive and enthusiastic
about their subjects, paying careful attention to the opinions of the students.
The flow of teacher-student discourse seemed never to be interrupted by
blank, sullen stares of disinterested pupils or disjointed ramblings from an
obviously unprepared instructor. This foray into my future school's academic
machinations made a big impression on me — I was excited and awed, pri-
vately wondering whether I would be able to contribute to the intellectual
give and take which the students engaged in with such facility.

The last class we went to was algebra — a hateful topic to me. No round
tables here, just rows of chairs, sullen, blank stares, and what seemed like
disjointed ramblings about quadratic equations. However, directly in front
of me and positioned by an open window was the most beautiful girl I had
ever seen or even tried to imagine. A deep tan, bleached blonde hair, and
very blue eyes were the first things I noticed about her. Later at lunch, I managed to overhear her chatting with, incredibly, several equally beautiful girls.
I was struck by the aggressive sophistication of their exchange. It was charged
with a confidence which gave me the impression that these sixteen-year-olds
were already women, having casually sidestepped the awkwardness of adolescence as if such a condition held no relevance to them.

As I reflect on that weekend visit, I know now that I had come no closer
in penetrating the illusion of the prep school experience than my repeated
examinations of the catalog. My brief exposure was punctuated by exhilarating overdoses of sight and sound. The sophisticated badinage between students at meals, the stunning campus, the prowess of the athletic teams — all
were powerful proof that this place seemed superior in every aspect.

This Edenesque portrait was exactly what was intended when the school
was created. Clearly its founders wished to ape their British ancestors across
the pond by sequestering the children of the "aristocracy" in an exclusive
schooling atmosphere which was a natural prerequisite for the inexorable
path toward leadership of society. The idea at my school was to emulate
English public schools the likes of Eton, Harrow, or Winchester — institutions of privilege bent on preserving privilege by being the only avenues to

power. The degree my school is an American replication of the English public school is striking. We did not belong in grades but in forms (6th form being the equivalent of 12th grade). The older buildings might as well have composed a quadrangle at Oxford. The teachers were "masters." Many students were legacies, and the Victorian adages of stiff upper lip, fair play, and staunch belief in one's class superiority were the accepted dogma.

After having more than one hundred years of practice, my school has perfected its role as an exclusive path to the best collegiate institutions – preparing its students to maintain the integrity of the Old Boy Network while blithely adding to, or creating wealth. Unlike the English system, where one's station as societal leader is in most cases unquestioned from birth, the absence of an aristocracy in America compelled our teachers to repeatedly remind us rather stridently that we were members of a gifted elite who must use our power for the good of the lower classes rather than the exploitation of them.

Outwardly, the school has been very successful in its mission. Out of privilege emerge intelligent, if not sassy, cosmopolitan eighteen-year-olds well prepared in an academic sense to bring any Ivy League school to its knees. Catalog compilers, parents, and trustees proudly point to each class's stunning college matriculation lists as evidence that the system works. The numbers are indeed impressive. Out of my class of one-hundred-and-fifty students, eighteen went to Harvard, fourteen to Yale, twelve to Princeton, nine to Brown, five to Dartmouth, and even thirteen heretics to Stanford.

When I finally arrived at my school as a student, it was remarkable how quickly my illusions of what prep school would be like collided with the reality. It was as if I had eagerly gone out on a sheet of ideal looking ice only to crash through and be engulfed by brutal and dangerous water. A contributing factor was the fact that I had been placed in a dorm (I'll call Dervey) which contained a volatile collection of the worst elements on campus. However, what is important about Dervey's residents is that they and the deeds they perpetrated were not anomalies in the fabric of the school's social structure. Rather, they were the leaders of the school, and their destructive attitudes were not shunned but revered and replicated. Therefore, though my Dervey experiences were perhaps exaggerated if compared with those of other new students in different dorms, sadly, they were not different enough.

After settling in, my first few days in Dervey were innocent ones, crammed with meetings with other new students and pep talks from various faculty members. But once old and new students began the routine of school life, the new students were no longer treated with deference – we were rudely booted out of the nest and expected to fly. This was what I expected and therefore didn't mind when the artificial kindness evaporated from my interaction with the veterans. However, what I was expected to do to earn my wings was something that, at the time, terrified me.

It began one evening when a knock on the door heralded the entrance of a contemporary to whom I had not yet spoken. I knew he was old because he had been pointed out as one of the "In-Crowd." He was stocky and unattractive, with oversized sleepy eyes, a pouting lower lip, and bad skin. Like all the arrogant and exclusive In-Crowders, he wore a black, heavy men's overcoat, army fatigues, and work boots. Such a wardrobe may have been preposterous looking, but it added mystique to those who were allowed to wear it.

Surveying my room with a cold eye, he sneered at its inadequacies (no expensive stereo, Grateful Dead tapes, or fern plants). Feeling inadequate myself, I nervously stared at the floor, but felt cheered when he walked over to examine my prized Jimi Hendrix poster.

"You like Hendrix?" he mumbled.

"Sure," I chirped eagerly, hoping we had found something to talk about.

"He wasn't bad for a boofer" (later I realized this was our school equivalent for the term "nigger"). "Nothing like getting stoned to Hendrix . . . you know what I mean?"

"No," I said, sensing an ominous turn in events.

"Really," he said with a weird kind of laugh that sounded more like a donkey's bray (and which I soon learned was practiced by all those In-Crowders); "Well, come to my room later on and we'll get stoned to Hendrix."

This invitation led to, in the argot of our school, a new student's choice to be "corrupted." More specifically, it was a rite of passage which any new student had to undergo in order to be considered eligible the following year to become, if not a member, then at least respected by the In-Crowd. A word more about this group: quite simply, they were those old students from whom the rest of the school sought approval. This was because they seemed to possess superhuman qualities. They were attractive yet incredibly snide commanders of all aspects of school life. They had done, and continued to do it all with astonishing gusto — sex, drugs of every description, enormous quantities of booze, histrionics in Boston while visiting siblings and friends at Harvard. Most incredibly, through their constant stupors of drug or alcohol intoxication, they managed to do well in class and at extracurricular activities.

If I was to make that journey across the hall and partake in the inhalation of "weed," I would, if I were lucky, take my first baby steps from "corruption" toward the coveted group. But at that moment, much to the astonishment of the In-Crowder, I politely declined. You see, I was most interested in preserving my sense of control. The idea of exchanging that control for what was then an unfamiliar experience terrified me to the degree that it was worth insulting the lascivious overtures of an In-Crowder.

In the weeks that followed, I was repeatedly invited to "corrupt" myself ("Want to have a smoke?;" "Let's do shots before dinner"), as if my first rebuke had been seen as a mistake on my part which I was being given a chance to rectify. But my common sense and fear of addling my brain kept me away from many a den of iniquity. This was my death warrant in Dervey house. Feeling threatened by my refusal to play ball, the veterans, almost to a person, ostracized me. I was the object of petty attempts at hazing such as vandalism, continuous verbal abuse of a highly sophisticated and brutal fashion, as well as feigned sexual attacks (my bad-skinned friend liked to threaten me with his penis as I tried to negotiate the urinal). Though these incidents tended to wear down one's constitution, I refused to cave in. I found refuge with some other disillusioned new students, and together we mocked the In-Crowders, though the reins of power remained far from our grasp.

Hazing annoyed and occasionally humiliated me, but what irked me about Dervey was the fact that none of the adults had any idea of the degree the dorm was beyond their control. Here, in bold-faced print, was the division between myth and reality. The faculty saw engaging young overachievers charging their way up the ladder of success. We were viewed as independent and responsible young adults capable of taking care of ourselves. But in fact, the school in general, and Dervey in particular, housed many who acted with wild irresponsibility toward themselves and others. All that was necessary to dupe the faculty in Dervey was to be subtle in one's intake of substances and address the faculty with a smile and a few obsequious salutations.

The dorm president was a master at this game. Quick of tongue and stern in manner, he was an oleaginous sycophant of the highest order. With calm assurances, he lied through his teeth in presenting the status of the dorm to the faculty member who supposedly was in charge. This teacher was spineless and uninvolved, never bothered by the antics around him unless they reached such a crescendo that he would have to open his door and tell the dorm president to quiet things down. I'll never forget our president's ability at dorm meetings to present our behavior as being nothing less than respectable. With confidence and swagger, he would talk of charity work or plans for the next dance in noble terms. Others, with their confidence and swagger, would chime in, and as students pretended to be interested in helping the homeless, the faculty beamed with satisfaction. Yet, this seemingly mature dorm president would, out of sight of adults, turn his plastic smile into a more accustomed sneer.

One evening, I asked him to help out with an incident involving my rug and a student nicknamed "Torch" because in a stoned reverie he had lit his bed on fire. That afternoon, Torch had entered my room so drunk he didn't want to bother to go to the bathroom, but urinated on my rug instead. As the stain before my incredulous eyes grew, I watched as this pathetic person's face twitched more than usual (it always twitched a little due to, word had it, too much cocaine). He passed out with a giggle, sagging face first into his newly created puddle. Upset, I asked the dorm president what he was going to do about this incident. With several mates languidly draped on his bed, he replied from a lotus position in front of his illegal television that he would "look into it." Sensing that the atmosphere was not conducive to further inquiries, I turned and left. Upon shutting the door, a chorus of derisive howls erupted from within. I felt totally alone and resolved to get out of Dervey any way possible.

My chance came when a student was kicked out, opening up space in another dorm. But I didn't get to move until after I had repeatedly appealed to the top authority figures at the school. To avoid implicating specific people (and thus be shunned by all students friend or foe), I relayed in general terms how the quiet exterior of Dervey was in fact a place of cruelty to those who wouldn't play ball and destructive for all. I told of one particular orgy of destructiveness precipitated by a "run" for booze to Boston by two sixth-formers. Armed with two trunks and two thousand dollars, they went to "town" and plundered a sleazy liquor store near South Station. All that evening, as the alcohol was consumed, a dangerous and evil atmosphere prevailed as one new student, desperate to please, collapsed in his own vomit while others followed suit.

I was granted my wish but not because of what I relayed about Dervey. Beyond a tepid effort to investigate, headed off by our intrepid dorm president, the administration did nothing because they clearly did not believe me. They refused to accept that such widespread drug and alcohol abuse was happening daily two hundred yards from their offices. They refused to believe that certain members of the powerful athletic teams were budding coke-heads or alcoholics. Perhaps, they undoubtedly mused, unsophisticated white trash from the local high school fell prey to such mundane afflictions, but certainly not future Ivy Leaguers!

On one level, my experience in Dervey was terrifying because I had never been exposed to drugs and their various negative ways of impacting human behavior. Neither had I seen a person with alcohol poisoning helplessly draped over a toilet bowel. As an adult, having seen all these things replicated at college, I am no longer terrified, but simply bored with such displays of human excess. However, prep school was, in my mind, not supposed to be an arena for such vigorous and prodigious drug and alcohol abuse (which in terms of drugs, at least, easily surpassed the amount of usage at my college). In this sense, my illusions about prep school were quickly and at times shockingly crushed.

But the drugs and drink in Dervey were merely a symptom of the greater problem. That problem was the attitude established and propagated by the In-Crowd elite and adopted by so many students. It was the attitude of supreme confidence in one's social superiority both in the context of the school and in the world beyond the school gates. Getting high was one major form of demonstrating this attitude that one was beyond the clutches of silly school regulations. But far worse, it was an attitude which spawned a feeling that one was unaffected by traditional rules of social decency — the cynical manipulation of people and situations for personal gain rather than comity and good will. If one refused to adopt "the attitude," one suffered the worst humiliation of all — that is, to be frozen out by many of one's peers and relegated to the status of non-person — a cipher viewed as having no relevance to campus life. Of course, not all students were part of this snobbish elite, and many non-persons were able to do well and make friends. But the power structure was such that because the Derveyites set the tone, which so many other students tried to emulate, it was inevitable that "the attitude" would permeate the campus.

A memorable example of "the attitude" in action, in terms of the cynical manipulation of a situation for one's personal gain, occurred during my last year at the school. A good friend I'll call Ted had in the previous winter managed to break his neck while skiing at an area local to the school. Permanently paralyzed from the chest down, he nevertheless recovered very quickly and returned in our sixth form fall to finish his career at the school with his class. Though confined to a wheelchair, he displayed admirable degrees of strength and aplomb in negotiating the disheartening realities of his new and unfortunate circumstances.

After we had all completed our college applications, a friend told me an incredible thing. A girl she knew had chosen to write about Ted in her Yale essay which asked one to describe the most influential event in one's life. This girl I'll call Lisa wrote, according to my girl friend, with heartfelt emotion about how devastated she was in the wake of Ted's accident, how close they had been, and how Ted's remarkable strength infused her with wisdom and hope. According to my friend, it was an emotional yet well-written piece which surely served to distinguish Lisa's most influential event from the thousands of others Yale officials would read about that year. I told Ted of this and he laughed derisively. Confused, I asked him what was so funny, and he informed me he found it odd how influential he could be in people's lives. He said he felt like a celebrity. I finally understood, for it turned out Ted didn't know Lisa from a hole in the wall. She had appropriated his disaster for her own purposes — a shining example of how "the attitude" could facilitate such cynical fraud. It reminded me of the kind of fraud regularly perpetrated by the Dervey president — seemingly earnest while simultaneously plotting how to take advantage. This whole incident made me wonder how many other essays were profiting from Ted's accident. Perhaps Lisa's was not the only one.

At my school, the hedonistic tumult of the Dervey era receded somewhat after my first year when many of the most influential students were either kicked out or graduated. However, the In-Crowd spirit prevailed represented by less aggressive but equally brutal clientele. They had shattered my illusions about the prep school experience, but I adapted, made friends, and moved on. However, memories of the destructiveness of "the attitude" in its ability to so sharply delineate between the haves and have-nots will always taint my memories of the place. I think of the beautiful facilities, the great opportunities, and yes, really quality people; but then I think of the many eager new students who became corrupted not only by dope, but by snideness, dishonesty, and jadedness. I think how unfortunate it is that these qualities were the norm rather than the exception. I think of my Dervey president and see a similarity in his sneer with that of Michael Milken or Ivan Boesky. I don't think that in trying to emulate Eton, the school's founders had that in mind.

9

Our Friendships Flourished

by Zooey L. Cato

"I hate you, I hate you! From now on we can't be friends! We can only be roommates, nothing more, never friends again! Never!" As a tenth-grader, these words stung. They were dealt at the climax of an intense argument with my first roommate at boarding school. Never before had I been in a truly nasty fight with a friend. Then again, I had never lived in such close proximity, nor spent so many waking and sleeping hours with anyone as I had with Liza. Prior to this argument, we had gotten along beautifully.

We had clicked from the start. The first day at prep school, in fact, we had eaten our farewell lunch together with our parents, and talked and laughed throughout the entire meal. Ironically, our parents had been more reserved during the course of our "Last Supper" together, while my roommate and I chatted like two busy bees, albeit jittery and nervous ones, who could not contain their wandering eyes. We absorbed our surroundings and the sea of foreign, but soon to be intimate, faces.

Only that morning I had pulled out of our stone driveway with my life piled into the station wagon. My throat had had a lump in it about the size of a tennis ball, and I had the same queasy feeling that an acrophobic gets when standing over a thousand foot precipice. Many anxieties churned in my stomach: "Am I ready to leave home?" "Will I be able to handle the academic pressure?" "Am I going to make friends?" "What will my roommate be like?"

When my parents and I arrived at my new home, we parked beside the brick dorm and walked up to my new room. A sticker posted on the door had my roommate's name, "Liza Dayton," on it with mine directly below. My clammy hands had difficulty grasping the knob, but I managed to push open the old wooden door. I surmised that the young, blond girl putting her clothes in the closet must indeed be Liza. Our parents greeted each other and shook hands while I whispered a meek "Hi" to this virtual stranger. The tennis ball lodged in my throat had meanwhile grown tenfold. We started hauling up my belongings and continued with the unpacking ritual. My eyes scanned my new roommate's desk on which rested a picture of her with another young girl with sandy blond hair. I picked up the frame and recognized a girl I had met that summer in my hometown. "I think I know that girl in your picture!" I said excitedly. " You know her?" she replied. "She's one of my best friends from home! We've gone to school together since first grade!" This connection, however minute, launched us into our first conversation. Our very separate worlds became joined, and from there we began to exchange more information about each other, learning that we had both shared the same apprehension about leaving home and making new friends. We discovered several other things in common that made us more at ease with each other as well as with ourselves. My twisted nerves gradually unwound as we hung up posters, put away clothes, and made our beds.

As the fall term progressed, Liza and I grew closer and closer, sharing not only clothes, jewelry, and even an occasional toothbrush, but also the emotional concerns that accompany adolescence. We shared more with each other than with anyone else at school, which as roommates was both easy and natural. Six nights a week we had study hall in our rooms for two hours after dinner. The first fifteen to twenty minutes we typically devoted to talk of male prospects, library happenings, and homework assignments. Although we had invariably had dinner only an hour or so before, we always managed to waste this early part of study hall. More talk, questions, and general thoughts mingled with homework until nine o'clock or so when we got antsy for our one officially designated half-hour of social interaction. From nine-thirty to ten, we had the option of venturing over to the snack bar "to see and be seen," or remaining at home in anticipation of that certain male visitor. In any event, nine o'clock usually concluded our studying for the night, as we spent the remainder of study hall weighing our social options and planning our own sort of mini-adventure.

From time to time, study halls offered greater excitement. One of the funnier events occurred when a friend got stuck under the bed because her chest was so huge! It happened around eight o'clock. I was not in my own room studying as I should have been, but in hers, probably pretending to do French homework together. For some reason she climbed under the bed on her back to retrieve a pen or something, and when she tried to climb back out, she couldn't get past her breasts! Of course, I was laughing so hard, and she was in such hysterics, squealing with laughter, that we didn't even think to lift up the bed. Our housemaster soon knocked. He opened the door only to see me crying with laughter and doubled over for fear of wetting my pants, and my friend's body shaking — half of it only — as her upper half was submerged. Our housemaster, of course, lifted the bed and angrily told her to get off the floor. But I could tell there was a hint of humor in his voice — how could anyone think that her predicament wasn't funny? What a memory: my good friend about 4'9", big mouth, big eyes, and a huge chest!

Another event that allowed for some spontaneity during study hall was the tradition that had started with coeducation, "the panty raid." Upper-class guys came into the lower-class girls' dorms during study hall, stole their underwear and bras, and hung them on bushes and trees around campus. It sounds harsh, and it was, especially if someone found a pair of your undies a week later with your name sewn in, but on the whole it was fun. On one of these occasions, we girls decided to retaliate after the guys went yelling out of our dorm, panties in hand, disguised as bandits so we couldn't tell who was who. We decided to follow them over to their dorms to retaliate! I think I grabbed one guy's shorts before I was heaved over another one's shoulder and put into the shower — cold water, clothes, shoes, and all! A meeting of the entire school was called regarding that incident at which it was determined that "panty raids" were discriminatory against females. The assumption was that we were the weaker sex and could be taken advantage of. Much of the stuff was true in a way, but most of the girls involved were not bothered by it since it was a fun time that encouraged friendships, student interaction, and school spirit. Unfortunately, the next year the administration banned "panty raids" from the already meager list of privileges. This is the sort of experience I remember from my early years at boarding school. Sometimes it kills me to think how completely immature we were! But I guess we had to live up to our reputation as "fledglings" and take advantage of such silliness as much as possible.

Since the first week of school, people continually asked whether Liza and I had known each other from somewhere before. We were coined the Bobbsey Twins because we were always together. And when we heard about other roommates having problems, we felt sorry for them and thankful for the fact that we had been put together — that is, until December, when for seemingly no reason, she exploded at me and I exploded back. What had started as an insignificant criticism escalated into extreme verbal abuse. Never before had I let leash so many malicious remarks onto a friend, especially one as close as Liza was. However, neither of us had ever lived with anyone, and therefore, had never grown so close in such a short period of time.

We did not speak for twenty-four hours. Although this may not seem like a substantial amount of time, it was like centuries for two teenagers accustomed to talking together several hours a day. Also, because our parents were never present for immediate advise, consolation, or just an open ear, we had come to rely on one another for support. For most of us, our friendships at boarding school developed and matured sooner and to a much deeper level than those at home because nearly every hour of the day was spent in contact.

Indeed, my adolescent years, like most other people's, were arguably the most formative years of my life. Between the ages of thirteen and nineteen, my friends and I underwent such enormous changes, ones inherent in the maturation process. With the onset of adolescence, we underwent not only the obvious physical changes, but also faced the unprecedented emotional instability that accompanies this stage of growing up. We had to cope with new insecurities like breast development and pimples. More importantly, we wrestled with the intangibles of identity crisis, waning confidence, and conversely, a growing consciousness. As stated in the school viewbook: "The dormitory experience helps foster personal growth ... Significant lessons about cooperation and honesty are both learned and reinforced ... Students learn to live with each other and to be tolerant and considerate." It's really true, the learning takes place not only in the classroom, but twenty-four hours a day.

My friendship with Liza had prospered until our feud created a major setback. The single word "hate" caused such excruciating, numbing pain that only after I seconded her vicious words, did I feel the wind being sucked out of me. I later recoiled, collapsed on the bed, and cried for what at the time seemed the loss of a best friend. During our twenty-four hours of silence, I suffered waves of nausea; every limb seemed to ache; every sound felt like it was crushing my brain. I yearned to retreat to my own room, my own space, somewhere, anywhere, just to avoid her. But I could not escape. The bare fact slapped me in the face: we lived together. We still had to sleep in the same room, brush our teeth at ten and wake up at seven.

Confrontation was extremely difficult and delicate to deal with at age fifteen. In fact, most of my friends shunned it. Such is the nature of teenage interaction and existence. In retrospect, this argument that reached its zenith with her cruel words, caused us to examine both ourselves and our friendships for the first time. We ultimately grew through our argument and subsequent period of silence. It both strengthened our ties and enhanced our own self-awareness. We learned about tolerance, sharing, respect for privacy, and perhaps most importantly, we learned how to communicate. True, we both clammed up for twenty-four hours, but then proximity took over, and we finally acknowledged our feelings.

During our day of silence, my roommate had received a package of grapefruit from Florida. She was peeling one when I reluctantly came back to the room for study hall. My gaze was averted downward as I muttered a "Hello" and lay down on my bed. Just when I was unsure of how I was going to concentrate on my math problems with her in the room, she broke the silence:

"Do you want a section?" I picked up my heavy head and turned to see her hand outstretched. The grapefruit's overflowing juices forced me to bend over the wastepaper basket beside her. Her peace offering evaporated the tension and we began anew. "I'm sorr ... I'm so ... sorry ... I really didn't mean for this to get so out of hand ..."

Only by actually living with someone would one have this encounter and be forced to come to terms not only with the other person but with oneself as well. Liza helped me realize my own shortcomings, and as a result, I grew to know myself better, became more comfortable with myself. The process was painful, but that's the price you pay for growing up.

At boarding school, friends take on other crucial, multi-faceted roles, primarily assuming that of a surrogate family. Away at school, I no longer had the immediate parental support often taken for granted by teenagers who live at home. Even the common cold, easily remedied by Mom, took on new meaning as a form of independent suffering. We all, at one time or another, had coughs, runny noses, and sniffles. Away from home, friends assumed the parental role of caring for our maladies.

For two consecutive winters, I had the misfortune of coming down with bronchitis. The first year, I coped for a few days in my dorm room. My roommate, as well as other friends, brought me meals, mail, and medicine. I would be lying on what I thought was my deathbed, with pallid face, dried-out lips, and cotton mouth when attentive friends came to check on my status and cheer me up with jokes and stories. They also filled me in on the gossip and the daily happenings — so much different from home where Mom and Dad were the only people I saw. Maybe a friend would call, but the conversations were invariably cut short by Mom ordering me to get off the phone and get some rest.

Sickness at boarding school thus became yet another bonding experience, particularly when someone else suffered at the same time. It became an all-day recess when two of us decided to "red-card" together (that is, go to the infirmary, claim or feign ill health, thereby being excused from classes for the day). Imagine two teenage girls surrounded by used tissues and cough syrup, vegetating in front of the T.V. switching channels: "What's on next, huh?" "I think 'Happy Days' or 'Wheel of Fortune' What do you want to watch?" "I don't care, as long as we see 'Days of Our Lives' later!" "Okay, I'm going to boil some more water for tea. Do you want some?"

Once again, time and circumstance joined two people who shared thoughts, feelings, and problems while everyone else attended class. Another dimension thus solidified and intensified this friendship, one that most teenagers who live at home never encounter. True, two sick college students can also "potato" in front of the T.V., however, they never receive the same satisfaction as prep schoolers do from having duped authority. Besides, in college, everyone at one point or another skips class because of an evil hangover.

Boarding schools are notorious for their overabundance of rules and regulations. My prep school not only lived up to this stereotype, but as many students would argue, the school exceeded the norm. The school's handbook, for instance, rivals a Tolstoy novel in its lengthy, detailed enumeration of rules and regulations. When a student's conduct and actions are so strictly governed, someone is bound to slip and step on a crack. Again, consider the age. We teeter on a tightrope that bridges puberty and adulthood. Coming into my school, we were thrust into an environment stripped of parental support and all made to conform. The pressures paralleled an investment banking job with "Broadcast News" time constraints. But even the supposedly straight-laced, impeccably dressed, and brainy boarding school student contains within himself the innate adolescent desire to rebel. This is often a teenager's way of testing the unknown.

Everyone at boarding school basically follows the same schedule. The school pulsates at a singular rhythmic beat. We wake up, eat breakfast in the same dining hall, attend classes, eat lunch, attend more classes, go to sports or drama practice, shower, eat dinner, study, and go to bed. Of course, I've consolidated the boarding existence a bit, but this certainly approaches an accurate outline of daily life. Activities may vary within different organizations, but everyone is essentially woven together by one common thread, namely the regimented schedule imposed by the school. The interactions at boarding school are therefore intense, especially when compared to the diffuse nature of collegiate life.

At times, however, we became so self-absorbed that we forgot others' worries, problems, and concerns. The only structured support systems were the senior proctors, the corridor masters, and the advisors. Although every student had these forms of guidance, friends became the major source of support.

My prep school, like any other top boarding school, had more than its share of academic pressures. The work overload was yet another common denominator in our lives and one that solidified friendships immensely. Pulling an "all nighter" was just one of the bonding experiences I first endured as an eleventh-grader. During the winter, when we all struggled to research and compile a fifteen-page paper on a topic in United States history, these all-nighters became a common occurrence. If you were fortunate enough, as I was, someone else would also be suffering from an incomplete paper and deadline.

I admit my propensity to procrastinate. It seems that even when I set myself a personal deadline, there was always a little devil lurking inside telling me: "Noooo, you're paper isn't really due in February, at least not until the twentieth, don't you remember? So now, go and watch Thursday night T.V.!" So much for manipulation of the mind! Thus, I invariably set myself up for many cups of black coffee and bloodshot eyes.

Fortunately, several days before the paper was due, my nocturnal activities coincided with one of my neighbor's. Part of the fun (if the word "fun" is at all appropriate) of a shared all-nighter were the breaks one took to release stress. One friend, Monica, and I have some memorable moments from our late-night study breaks. With only several days before my history paper was due, I suffered a severe mental block and was in the bizarre frame of mind that often characterizes brain overload. I could not bear the confinement of my room any longer, so stomped across the hall to Monica's room, collapsed on her floor and shrieked: "I can't take this any more! I'm going to go insane if I see another note card!" Although it was three in the morning, she was as caffeine-pumped and frenzied as I. Her desk bore a striking resemblance to mine — note cards, books, and crumpled paper cluttered the area. She hovered over her desk, wearing a bandanna tied Aunt-Jemina style around her head and sporting an old pair of sweats.

Suffering through the same pressure, she readily joined me on the floor, and we both lay sprawled and let loose two successive, shrill screams. Perhaps it was our unsightliness or maybe the realization of our crazed state, but we soon became drowned in uncontrollable laughter. Our heads were positioned opposite, such that we were looking at each other upside down. My eyes saw her chin, nose, and mouth inverted; she saw me the same way. We both started making absurd facial contortions — wrinkling our noses and moving our mouths into various positions. If you suffer from lack of laughter, I guarantee that staring into a friend's face from this vantage point will inject humor into your day. Then again, one really has to be in the frame of mind for it, as she and I were that night. We must have been on her floor for fifteen minutes releasing all our pent up energy and frustration through these absurd antics.

At home, one does not have this means of release. Brothers and sisters, unless in the same grade, do not usually undergo academic stress simultaneously. Distance and curfews simply prevent adolescents from engaging in such late night lunacy. The telephone does not compare to kicking your legs wildly about with a friend, having a water gun fight, or blasting music and singing as loudly as possible to "The Police".

Meals were another bonding experience. Indeed, dining at my school was probably the biggest social extravaganza going. First, everyone was always there. We had to be, school rules required it. Second, the time allotted for meals was a meager forty-five minutes for lunch and seventy-five for dinner. Given a total span of two hours in which to eat and socialize, we all milked the most out of every moment. I vividly remember lounging around the table long after finishing a meal. We ventured over to other tables to chat, sometimes even mustering up the courage to visit a "special" male friend's table. The various social groups sat in their self-designated areas of the dining hall. You never sat near the salad bar unless you were a teacher's pet; you sat in the back if you were cool and by the exit if you were a deadhead. The latter half of the dining period likened to a gaggle of chatty geese. Everyone mingled with robust intensity, for it was virtually the only time the two genders could interact on a large scale basis.

Conversation typically centered around the day's athletic events, evolving relationships, etc., much akin to the high school lunchroom scene. The boarding school conversation, however, differed from high school and especially talk at home primarily in terms of social content. Who at a day school, for instance, could relate stories about pulling a prank at four in the morning or going on a midnight panty raid? Meals at boarding school thus served as a unique vehicle for social interaction — interaction not based on partying or dancing, but just open, healthy conversation.

Another opportunity for communal eating was the "feed." "Feeds" happen when teenagers eat fresh, non-institutional food cooked by themselves or a faculty member. Fellow hall members decide on the food group — usually sweet and seldom healthy. I recall the most outstanding feed of my boarding school experience — a scrumptious cheese and chocolate fondue. Hhmmmmmm . . . thick, warm, gooey cheese and rich melted chocolate dipped in strawberries, a welcome bombardment of the senses beyond compare. With Cat Stevens playing in the background, we had a cheese-stretching contest to see who could make the longest string. I think the winner stretched it to eight feet or so. We slowly savored the luscious fondue until no remnants of our feast remained. After dinner and dessert, the eight of us lay sprawled out on the floor, weary from the combination of meal and laughter. Topics of conversation ranged from parents, emotional and academic problems to many of the small joys we had experienced in the course of the day. Perhaps at home it would have been just another one of Mom's meals, good tasting, but largely taken for granted. How in the world could you enjoy such a delicious meal (and actually appreciate it!) and laugh so much at the same time?

Several feeds, all-nighters, and papers later, my roommate and I embraced at graduation and drenched each other with tears. Our original homes, as well as our college plans, would cause our paths to diverge. She would go south and I would go north. Would we make new friends who would weaken our longstanding friendship? When would we see each other again? Would our paths cross? The hug's intensity increased; we did not want to let go, fearing a part of our life being sucked away.

Another friend honked her horn; there was a train to catch. I grabbed my friend's hand and stole away up the stairs to our very first room. We thrust ourselves through the heavy wooden door where three years before we had crossed the threshold to our teenage rites of passage. We furiously carved our names into the closet door: "Friends Through Eternity: 1988."

10

Loneliness

by Josiah Stone

When I look back to write about my experiences at prep school, I feel a lot of guilt. My school is regarded as the cream of the crop. The smartest, the richest, and the most influential families want their kids to get in. The Alumni include such notables as G.B. Trudeau, Hobie Baker and movie stars like Catherine Oxenberg and Judd Nelson. Graduation speakers have ranged from Gary Hart to T. Berry Brazelton and even Desmond Tutu. Our athletes have started for the Boston Bruins and won Gold in the 1988 Summer Games. In my class alone twenty-three went to Harvard University, and of the one hundred twenty-five, roughly 85% went to Ivy League schools, Stanford and MIT included, while the others went to schools like Wesleyan, Amherst, Middlebury, and Williams. Of course, everyone graduated; that was a given, and very few took the year off because they didn't get into a college they wanted to attend. Lastly, the school's endowment, except for, I think, the University of Texas, is higher per student than any high school or college in the country. Basically, we were constantly reminded that we were the best, and our opportunities and environment reinforced that idea.

This brings me to why I feel guilty and nervous writing anything bad about a school that is perceived by most people to be "the best." Speakers always addressed us as the students who would be presidents and leaders of our country. So, who am I to fly in the face of history and suggest there are some weaknesses with one of the United States' greatest boarding schools.

My story deals with feeling like an outcast while at school. Whenever someone asks me if there was one problem with the school, I always say it was that they never let you know that you were okay just being normal or average. I think my problems stemmed from a combination of not joining in, and convincing myself that those who were "in," or popular, were the successful ones at the school. I figured that if I didn't fit in, I could circumvent this by being the best at something, earning respect, and then eventually fitting in. I wanted to be better than everyone to make up for my being an outcast. I wanted to be able to say: "Well,

I am better than they are anyway; who needs them!" So I put pressure on myself to succeed as a reaction to feeling that I didn't fit in.

What is meant by "success" in boarding schools? Am I talking about grades, college admission, sports, and class elections? Yes. However, success also includes areas that don't go in college brag lists. Success is the guy who has the good-looking girl friend, the guy who can get away with smoking the most dope, and the snob who knows how to make others feel insecure and angry. Success for me was synonymous with respect, and I felt I had to get it to either fit in or to rationalize why I wasn't fitting in.

My first experience at school remains with me and was not pleasant. I quickly found out that freshmen were called "newbs" or new boys. Subsequently, those who were not known to be outstanding before they got there — the recruited hockey player, the beautiful freshman girl, or the alumnus' son, who was wined and dined by the faculty member (who was buddy-buddy with his famous father) — were subjected to "newb" abuse or hazing. It was late one night in the dorm, and my roommate and I were almost asleep when I heard yelling and running in the hall. All of a sudden our door was flung wide open, and there was a sea of laughing faces. They yelled something about being a newb and then threw a bunch of water balloons into our room. Most of them destroyed the posters on the slanted walls, and the water dripped down on our beds below. Then there were several irritating sounds: falling glasses that held my change and pencils and a vase breaking as it hit the floor. It felt like a rape of my possessions. After all was said and done, there was one balloon still intact. I told my roommate that we should go and get them back, but he said not to worry, we'd be better off doing nothing. I said: "Screw that," and ran downstairs and opened the door to the room of two of the seniors I knew had been involved. Their faces were stunned with disbelief. I was so angry, there was never any doubt that I was going to throw the balloon. I just wanted to pause to make those two jerks know how horrible I had just felt when they had done the same to me. I waited, which added to my feeling of sweet revenge, and then threw it as hard as I could right at them. Not staying to see the result or their reaction, I ran back upstairs. The only difference in our actions was the consequence. The seniors later told some other people in the dorm what I had done, and the upperclassmen started to ignore or tease me. At a day school or regular high school, I would have had the opportunity to go home or spend the afternoon with a best friend. However, since I was at boarding school, these were the people I would be eating, sleeping, and studying with and competing against for the next year, at least. I felt trapped in a situation in which I would be forced to make friends with a bunch of complete jerks. I couldn't understand that this was the way new people were treated. Why did being a freshman have to be such a tough adjustment?

This experience led me to become more introverted. I was scared to challenge the "popular" world of the upperclassmen because, if I did, I would have a hard time making friends. My whole freshman year went on, and I did not have much respect for these people. Actually that would be a mature way of looking at it. The fact is I did not like these guys. I felt everyone was nice to me on an individual basis, but in a group, they tended to make fun of me because I was new. That was when I began to drop out of school mentally and try to figure out a way to survive.

Almost every day during the week there were chapel services. Being a Jew probably didn't help my fitting in (there were five of us in the school), and I was never sure whether to pray, chant, do both, or none at all. However, the more I went to chapel, the more I noticed that the rector, or whoever, would recognize those people who had been honored in some way. He would either announce the people who had been named all-Americans, or those individuals who had won the debate over the weekend, or people who had been selected as merit scholars based on their board scores. After listening to these awards day after day, I realized this was a way to prove myself and, at least, gain respect, if not acceptance. I was going to prove I was better than those guys who had treated me badly.

I had an advisor, but didn't feel comfortable talking with him about the way I was being treated by other students. Maybe it was because I felt wimpy saying it, or more likely, it is hard to be intimate with someone who is assigned to you. The whole idea was too impersonal for me. My freshman year, my "Godfather," a faculty member, who was supposed to answer questions and orient freshmen to the school, never contacted me, and my advisor was an old math teacher who was not a communicator. I admit, I may be demanding, but teachers in boarding school should be able to tell when things are not going well. I remember how my advisor asked me into his office for ten minutes before the house master's reports were due so he would have something to say about me in his report to my family. My folks would read this blurb and probably think I was having a great time. So without many friends and no one to care about how I was doing, I decided to care for myself and prove them wrong. I was an angry, scared, lonely kid determined to succeed.

My pressure to succeed was not necessarily caused by the school. It was a reaction to a feeling of isolation which came from being ostracized. I was unwilling to assimilate into a system I didn't believe in. Thus, I decided to work hard as a means to rationalize the horrible time I was having. As you can guess, this was not a healthy atmosphere for me. After dinner, when friends would gather and chat, I would go back to an empty dorm and start to work. Even if I only had a simple exercise to do in French, I would treat it like a thesis and be extremely meticulous. Sadly, as the school year progressed, I became more and more introverted and used this system of working hard as a security blanket. I would kid myself and say: "Well, I'll just wait 'til the summer for fun and then have a normal time."

When my father came up to school, I used to invite a friend out to dinner. I did this for two reasons. First, it protected me from breaking down and telling him how I was really doing. By having someone there, the conversation never became intimate, so I was able to avoid dealing with the truth. Second, I thought it would help me gain friends. If I did something nice for them, then maybe they would be nice to me. In boarding school, I found there was never really a support system to help get me involved. I wasn't strong enough to reach out for help, definitely not more than once, and consequently, my pressure to succeed became more a matter of survival.

The fact is there was pressure, but the hard part of any obstacle is having to do it alone, and at my school, loneliness was my real enemy. I never wanted to admit to myself that I was lonely. I could always play some game, read, draw, run, or whatever, but always alone, and this was my life preserver. I started to relive all the fun times of the past: the summer parties and the survival trips to Africa and South America. Here I was, only in ninth grade, already acting like a ninety-year-old man because my life was depressing, and I thought I could do nothing about it. Eventually I even felt a bit mechanical around people because I did not know how to act. How can you be yourself when you don't even know who you are. For me, it is difficult to talk about how miserable my high school years were because I'm almost embarrassed. While in school, I would always hear wild stories from my friend at another boarding school about what a great time he was having, or else I'd go to a teenie-bopper movie about high school and see it portrayed as so normal and fun.

To be honest, at the time, I never thought of myself as an outcast, however, I did feel lonely very often. Loneliness is a tough situation to escape from. If you're fat, you exercise; if you're failing, you study; but if you're lonely, it is difficult to remedy on your own. I realized I was lonely because I would spend a lot of time drawing, reading, or running by myself. It got to the point where I would cringe when there were mandatory social settings. I never had that one friend to hang out with. I often went into town by myself and would just explore. It was one of the only ways of doing something new.

An experience I remember vividly was the "formal." In most other high schools in the country, there is the senior prom. For better or worse, it happens to every senior. There have even been movies portraying it as an important event in everyone's life. My school did not have a prom. Instead, my sophomore year, there was a spring formal. I remember how much terror this caused me. First of all, I had no date, although this was not uncommon. But what I remember most was being in this guy's room, and he and his roommate were going to the formal and asked if I was going, and I remember saying how I did not like that kind of thing and was just going to hang out. But I also remember how much anxiety I felt about not having the proper attire, not being able to look cool —

which was preppy at my school, and the fear that if I went, I would have nobody to hang out with or talk to. Deep down, though, I wish those guys had forced me because I knew everyone else was going, even the "losers."

Instead, I watched all my dormmates walk to the formal, and I went back to my room and sat down. This was one of the saddest moments in my life because as I sat there, I came out of my self-absorbed shell and realized that everyone in the whole school was at this "fun" event, and I was here in my third floor dingy dorm room reading "Sports Illustrated" all alone. For the first time in my life, I realized I was alone and that nobody really cared where I was. I had no friends who asked about me. My advisor certainly didn't check to see if I had gone; no one in the dorm cared if I went. Not even my parents called to see if I understood that, although they loved me deeply, they could not help me now. It was at this point that I actually felt sorry for myself and realized how miserable my life was at school. I think I even cried. I also felt anxiety when later everyone returned laughing and talking, while I had had the worst evening of my life. I had to fool them. If they spoke to me, I not only had to convince them I had had a good time, but also had to be "cool" in the way I did it. For me, loneliness is having to pretend that you are having fun by yourself, even though you know you are not. Loneliness is a way of occupying your time so you don't have to face the fears of reality: the girl who dumped you, the class bully, or in my case, not fitting in.

Once a year the school invited parents to come up and see what the school was doing. It was a chance to see where all their money was going. Prior to my attending prep school, Parent's Day had always been a proud moment for my mom and dad because they would usually hear how much of a joy I was to have in class and how well I was doing. Even in my worst of academic years, my parents would hear that I was having too good a time and that I should be doing more studying, that I was not a serious enough student.

Well, at my prep school, not being serious enough was never the problem. In fact, my experience was all too serious, and it came to a climax during Parents Weekend of my sophomore year. I can remember feeling nervous that my parents were coming up because I knew how brutally honest my mother could be in "calling a spade a spade." My father, although I love him, was not the great communicator and especially with the likes of what he was going to face that weekend. I knew he wouldn't be a problem because he would never make me talk, but my mother was another story. She would make me discuss the things I didn't want to. I knew she could, and would, hit all my sensitive spots. Just thinking about it made me sweat with anxiety and fear.

The weekend was going fine. We had gone to all the events, and I was able to comfortably answer "yes" and "no" to their questions. However, I could tell we were not having the same parents weekend experience as the other kids. I always felt we were walking around as the three of us. The other family groups were meeting their children's friends, going out to dinner together, and learning all about the many activities their children were involved in. However, with me, we just kind of walked around without really talking about me in relation to friends or classes. Rather, we would discuss summer or vacation plans which was fine with me because it never touched any sensitive areas.

However, on Sunday, all hell broke loose. Although I hadn't known it, I had been dying to tell my parents what I was really feeling because if there was anyone I could share my feelings with, it would have to be them. Anyway, we had gone into town for lunch before they went home, and I guess I was feeling kind of relieved because it was the longest period of time that I had talked with someone all year. Even though we hadn't spoken "truths," I still kind of liked the idea of being with people without feeling threatened. On the way up Main Street, my mother started asking me those questions I didn't want to hear. "How are you getting involved in the school — besides sports?" "Why don't you do debating or public speaking; it would be good for you." As the questions came at me harder and faster, I was beginning to have a difficult time fighting her off with "I don't know," and "Let me do what I want." She made me get involved in my answers, and I could sense a lot of feelings getting ready to burst. I remember sitting in the back of our Buick Riviera. It gave me a comfortable feeling to be inside this car I had spent so much time in growing up. It reminded me of the fun I used to have in my earlier years. However, I couldn't escape by day dreaming. My mother continued to probe and question. I finally began to break down.

"Just leave me alone!" I screamed. "Just drop me off and you can go home!" It was almost as if I was trying to give my mother a guilt trip for deserting me at school and letting me suffer.

"Let you go back to school? Why? As far as I can see, you aren't doing anything there! It's an absolute waste of time and money," she screamed.

"Well then, drop me off and let me do nothing; it's better than talking to you."

"You don't talk to anyone; you don't belong at this school; you're not like the other kids. I don't see that you have any friends here."

"Don't say that, honey," my Dad interjected. "It seems like he has a lot of nice kids to be friends with." For some reason, that comment angered me no end. How could he judge the kids in my school?

"You don't know!" I screamed at the top of my lungs. "I hate it here. The only reason I'm here is 'cause you decided it was the best school to go to! I can't wait 'til I graduate; then, at least I'll be free. You can go home and do whatever you want, but I'm stuck here." Then I started to cry, and I said sobbing: "I wish I had never come here." That statement summarized all my feelings. Being with my parents for the weekend had made me feel like a prisoner on leave for two days. My breaking down as we drove back to the school was not a coincidence. I didn't want to go back. I wanted to go home.

It was at this point that the tone of the argument switched. No longer was the issue about getting involved; it was clear that my happiness was at stake.

A sixteen-year-old kid should be enjoying school, not suffering through it every minute.

My mother said: "I don't want you to go back; enough is enough. Maybe we can see if you can transfer to another boarding school or even to the public high school." I can remember crying uncontrollably and I felt some comfort in her words, "I never realized you were this miserable."

For the next twenty-five minutes, we sat in the car, thirty yards outside the front entrance to the school with the bold letters of its sign staring at us as if reminding us that this institution was too high-powered for mere children. It's hard to remember exactly what got resolved. I think it was that I would stick it out the rest of the term and transfer if things were still bad. So, I went back to my room and sat down. I felt kind of good about the fact that now my parents shared my plight and sympathized with what I was going through. It was the first time I felt a little less lonely; someone else understood.

In retrospect, my experience at prep school is rather ironic. I have just completed looking for a job, and the expression that all of the bank training programs use is "a good fit." They want someone who is going to "fit into their culture." Consider a two-thousand-person bank meticulously choosing its potential Loan Officers based on "a good fit" in terms of personality when a 500 person, closely-knit community like my prep school couldn't help everyone fit in. It's almost as though the banks know that in order to produce successful people, it is more important to have eager, intelligent, energetic employees who fit in than only "the brightest" and "the best educated." Maybe that is why some banks are so much more successful than others, and some prep schools so much more successful in some ways than mine. While some academies did not get twenty-three of their seniors into Harvard, maybe their graduates who went to "lesser" colleges had a happier, richer adolescence. It's funny because some of the bank programs I applied to hire fifty people knowing that twenty-five will be fired because they want to keep only the best. Others said: "We know that certain programs like that exist, but we are dedicated to all fifty of our trainees and know that the training will be tough." But instead of saying: "You're on your own to sink or swim," they feel your success in this program is as much their responsibility as it is yours. Looking back, I can see which attitude my school exercised.

My prep school believed that sticking the best students in the country together with the best teachers, the best facilities, the most opportunities, and the most money would mold the best possible students. Make no mistake, every student had a special reason for being there. They were either extremely intelligent, or excelled in some other tangible area, or were simply the children of wealthy alumni contributors. My gripe is not with the idea of having the best students. That is, of course, what every school, college, and company strives for. The fault, however, lies in the failure to recognize that this is a delicate period in one's life. Not everyone is meant to be a star immediately. Even Michael Jordan did not start for his high school basketball team. People grow and improve at different rates, and my school failed to recognize this. I felt they worked more with the successes and left those of us who needed more time to work things out too much alone.

11

How Come We're Sick and Tired?

by Liza J. Sicard

Two years of boarding school and never sick a day of it! Never "officially" sick that is. I was constantly battling one cold or another, but I didn't allow myself to be ill. There was no time for sickness, no time for weakness. Despite the school operating a well-equipped infirmary, I never used their services and knew of only two students who took advantage of the facility. Sickness was a hassle, a roadblock in my busy preparation for the real world of college. There were certain dues associated with going to prep school. If we rested now, we'd pay later. So instead, we took our drugs, legal or illegal, and went to class. I was attending a prestigious prep school, and I believed that this "health" ritual was part of my preparation for life and college.

While at boarding school, I always felt I was one of the healthier students, and therefore better prepared than most to deal with the daily demands and succeed. The one area where I pushed myself beyond my limitations, though, was sleep. I could never get enough. After a full day of classes, afternoon athletics, and evening study hours, the schedule set by the school included eight hours of sleep from approximately eleven to seven each night. My body needed more, but I was lucky to get even that. Almost none of my friends got that much; none of us got it consistently.

After nine-thirty check-in, the school allowed juniors and seniors the "privilege" of unlimited lights. The T.V. and phone were off limits after eleven, but bedtime was our decision. It was a "privilege" few of us were well-prepared to handle.

At about ten, when check-in was complete and the dorm was quieting down, dorm parents returned to their apartments. They had finished their final duty in a long day of demanding responsibilities. They had work to do, and we could often see their lights burning long into the night. At no other time of the day was the dorm as alive with activity. We were all there and could finally spend time with friends. This casual contact wasn't built into our daytime schedule. We were free to move about as we wished, so common rooms were filled with students talking, eating, and studying together. Muffled voices could be heard behind locked doors where smoking, drugs, or sometimes sex was taking place.

We felt it was an academic and social necessity to stay up late. Some students didn't begin their homework until ten at night, choosing to sleep during study hours. But most of us had worked steadily and still had more to do. Unfortunately, we didn't just work. We procrastinated, gossiped, and complained about the amount of work we had. The assignments usually got done, but in twice the time required. Although we might not have been working our hardest, we were definitely working our longest. We felt we were working as hard as we possibly could. It was normal to stay up late because everyone in the dorm did. I felt guilty if I didn't put in lots of time. I wondered if I was working hard enough. I was afraid I might not succeed if I didn't keep putting in time. We weren't very productive or efficient during those late hours, but we were putting in our time, paying our dues.

Although alive with movement and activity, the dorm was generally quiet at night. Too much noise would awaken the few students who were sleeping. We were careful not to wake our dorm parents who might choose to enforce a lights-out policy. By two in the morning, the activity had usually ebbed, except for a group of all-nighters. These students weren't always the same, but their complaints were. They would bemoan their excess amount of work as their dormmates turned in for a few hours sleep. I couldn't help but feel a little guilty listening to them. I often wondered if I'd worked long enough. I respected the all-nighters for their dedication, but I needed some sleep.

Even then, I barely got enough sleep to keep me going. After a late night of studying, I always hoped for an afternoon nap, but there was no time. So I would work all week, often exhausted by Friday, and then "crash" every weekend. I'd go to bed by ten on Friday night, sleep till noon, go to brunch and then take an afternoon nap. If it wasn't an "academic" weekend (Saturday classes), I would get two days rest before the cycle began again on Monday. I often wanted to be more social on weekends and was impressed by those who were, but I was too tired. I was frustrated with missing the fun part of school life, but my body did not have the energy to party. I was paying my dues.

Vacations were even more frustrating. At the beginning of one vacation when I walked through the door of my house, my brother's first words to me were: "Why are you wearing purple eye shadow under your eyes?" I wasn't. I hadn't slept in two days. At school, knowing that a break was in the near future, I delayed sleep as much as possible so I could complete my work. I would tell myself: "I'll sleep when I get home." When I did finally get home, my body would break down. I spent much of my vacation either sleeping, eating, or taking aspirin. I usually had a cold by the second day and would just be getting over it by the end of vacation. I wanted to see friends and make up for lost partying time, but my body rebelled. When I finally allowed it to stop and rest a little, it would break down completely.

The worst vacations were the ones following exams: Thanksgiving and spring break. My first Thanksgiving vacation is a blur. I had just completed the first trimester of my junior year, my first exams, and my first all-nighter. Some students pulled all-nighters regularly, two or three a week even, but I only pulled them as a last resort.

I had completed my first day of exams and had begun to study for my U.S. history test that afternoon. I realized quickly I knew little. Three months of material, and I couldn't remember any dates. I was scared to death, scared of actually failing an exam. After the initial panic, I decided I had no choice but to study all night. So I walked down to the drugstore in town and invested in my first bottle of Vivarin. I knew I couldn't stay up without some help, and my help had to be legal.

As the rest of the dorm went to sleep about two in the morning, I was a member of the all-nighter group for the first time. I complained about how much studying I needed to do, and though I dreaded the upcoming hours, I enjoyed seeing the trace of respect in the eyes of my dormmates. My two friends, who had stayed up with me to provide support, also had a lot to do, but none of us would have pulled an all-nighter without the encouragement of the others. We were panicked about our exams. Since we were together, one person's anxiety played off the others' and multiplied. We insisted that pulling an all-nighter was an academic necessity, and doing it together would be more fun than trying it alone. So, the three of us studied all night in the common room.

We had a hot water pot for coffee and tea, and I donated a huge bag of pretzels so we wouldn't get hungry. We took study breaks to keep each other awake and in good spirits. At four, we started giggling over nothing in particular. Suddenly, everything was funny, and we laughed until our sides hurt. At five, I got the "jitters" and couldn't hold my pencil. My friends calmed me down, walked me around the halls, and wouldn't let me have any more caffeine until an hour before the test. At six in the morning, one of my all-nighter friends went running because if she didn't exercise, she would have fallen asleep. At seven, we all went to breakfast. It was the only breakfast I ever attended at school, and it was like watching the living dead — it looked like every student there had pulled an all-nighter. By then I knew all the U.S. history I would ever know, but I was still scared. I was scared of falling asleep during the exam or "blacking out." I'd heard of other students to whom these things had happened. So, I took another Vivarin and went to the exam. For a long tense minute after getting my paper, I didn't know a thing, but then my mind cleared and I did well.

The worst part of the all-nighter was not the long night or the day after, but the day after that. I still had one more exam to take. Fortunately it was in precalculus, my best subject. With the help of a sleeping pill that night and a Vivarin the next morning, I survived the test. But I barely survived the following five-day vacation. I considered leaving school that Thanksgiving. I didn't think I could endure the structure or the demands. But there was another part of me that felt proud. Sure, I was abusing my body, but I was not only coping but succeeding in this prep school. Wasn't that why I was there? And it would get easier, wouldn't it?

It never did get any easier, just more familiar. All-nighters, Vivarin, sleeping pills, and vacation colds became basic parts of my years in boarding school. I was successful, and I was "healthy" — I never missed a day of school.

While sleeping happened to be my addiction, every student had his own. Besides legal and illegal drugs, there was also food. Although the majority of students skipped breakfast, lunch and dinner were social events, and only homework could justify missing one of these meals. Attendance at meals was not mandatory, but meals were an opportunity to spend time with friends. I ate many meals of a peanut butter and jelly sandwich with three sips of tea. Other friends ate only desserts or liquid meals or multiple servings of Coke and coffee. We usually got enough of our most important "vitamin," caffeine, to prepare for a long evening of studying. Considering what I saw friends eat regularly, I would say that many students did not get enough nutrition. The food service offered balanced meals with a great deal of variety, but it was our responsibility to eat what was served. As teenagers, it was a responsibility for which some may not have been prepared. Unfortunately, our bodies paid the consequences. My senior year, the food service posted the entire daily menu with the calorie and fat content of each item. It was a well-intentioned idea, but it had its faults. I was surprised to see how many calories and how much fat was in the food I regularly ate. Their plan may have inadvertently reinforced the fear of gaining weight, thus the prevalence of dieting.

Fear of the "freshman fifteen" or the "boarding school bulge" was rampant among the females on campus. The popularity of fad diets, diet pills, and eating disorders grew out of this fear. With many teenage girls living closely together, comparisons of looks, clothes, and figures were unavoidable. We shared clothes, fixed each other's hair, and traded diet tips. No one wanted to get the "bulge," and some girls even wanted to lose weight. They would attend meals together, help each other exercise, and talk about losing weight. A few extra pounds seemed more important when thinner friends were dieting, so someone else would join "the club," and dieting multiplied throughout the female population on campus.

One girl I knew used to live on Dexatrim and salad. But eating meals was a social occasion not to be missed. So she would dress every night for dinner, fix herself a bowl of lettuce (no extras or dressing), and socialize for an hour.

She would pick from everyone's plate, but insist she wasn't hungry or didn't want any more. Her favorite topic of conversation was food. She could quote health facts about every food on the table along with calorie content. When a friend suggested she eat something in particular, she would say "No" and tell us how fattening it was.

Her dormmates tried to talk to her almost every night, and she'd talk about lots of problems in her life, but she would deny being anorexic. She'd tell them about wanting to be popular, her worries about grades, a boy she liked, or the coach who didn't think she was strong enough. Although she could talk nonstop about herself and food, she didn't believe she had an eating problem. Before going to sleep, she would examine her body in the bathroom mirror, pointing out microscopic bulges of fat to the other girls. Frustrated, they'd sometimes scream at her to notice the bones that stuck out or her pale skin color, and she'd yell back that they didn't understand.

Another girl arrived at school the same year I did, and we shared many common friends. The first year went smoothly for her, or so I thought. By the following fall, though, I knew she had bulimia. All her friends knew, and we felt guilty for not discovering it sooner. But bulimia is harder to detect than anorexia. She attended every meal, usually for the longest time possible. She would arrive at five in the afternoon for dinner and did not leave until after seven. During these two hours, she would socialize with everyone, as friends came and went, and eat non-stop. At first, she would bus her tray and then start over with another group, but as time went on, she would just let the dishes pile up as she devoured three entrees and five desserts. Periodically, she would take a casual break and sneak downstairs to the rest room to vomit.

In the evening, she would eat in the dorm and vomit there. Her dormmates, who hated the smell in the bathroom, knew she had a problem. She acknowledged her problem, but said it was under control. Friends spent a great deal of time talking to her and about her. It was new to many of them and difficult to cope with. They tried to help and counsel. One friend approached the peer counseling group and a few adults for advice, but not for assistance. They believed that only her friends could help her. Everyone had a different method, from yelling to pampering, to lots of talking. She was showered with concern and attention. People she barely knew wanted to help her. Even the yelling was attention.

I knew several girls with eating disorders at school, but few who got better. My best friend at home was anorexic, but that was easier to deal with than the eating disorders of casual school friends and acquaintances. She went home each night to a family who could help or hurt her. As her parents went through a bitter divorce, we blamed them for her problems. School and friends were her therapy. But the girls at boarding school didn't return to parents each night, and the absence of parents transferred the responsibility for dealing with the illness from her family to us. Boarding school life is all-encompassing. There is no place to hide. When you share classes, sports, friends, dorms, and bathrooms with the same people, it is difficult to keep any secrets or have any personal space. It's life under a microscope.

But these two people didn't have eating disorders when they arrived at school. Their problems were magnified in this microscopic environment, and so were our concerns. We were their friends and peers and should have been part of the therapy. But we were also the family they couldn't escape from — we were part of the problem. Because they were sick, friends showered them with care and concern, giving them the attention they so desperately wanted. An eating disorder meant increased attention and more friends, so they continued their disorder to continue the rewards. They were dependent on us for attention. We felt so important, but also so helpless because they were not getting better. Of course, we were victims too. Professional help would have told us not to reward the behavior but rather to reinforce the positive aspects of their personality, but we didn't listen to professional help. How could we turn our backs, ignore the problems, and pretend not to care about our friends' eating disorders. As friends, we felt we knew what was best.

These same two people were not star athletes, talented actors, class leaders, or brilliant students. Nevertheless, almost everyone on campus knew them or at least had heard about their individual problems. Surrounded by talented teenagers, recognition was quite an accomplishment. And all it took was an eating disorder.

A more common addiction that affected nearly every student was work. We stayed up late and skipped meals to study and earn good grades. We complained about our work load, our demanding teachers, and our difficult classes. We compared the time each of us spent on an assignment. More time meant more respect. It was part of paying our dues. Work was our epidemic illness, but some students took this addiction to the furthest extreme.

Another acquaintance arrived the same year I did and lived down the hall from me. I was impressed by her maturity and intelligence. I believed she had the world on her side, but by winter term, she had lost ten pounds and pulled frequent all-nighters. She didn't procrastinate as much as the rest of us and worked a lot longer. One day, she fainted in her room. Her roommate found her and took her to the infirmary. She was suffering from exhaustion. She had not been eating or sleeping regularly. They kept her for three days. When she was released she was three days behind in her work, so she cut meals and stayed up late to catch up. About a week later, she was out cold again. After three more days in the infirmary, she immediately returned to her habits when she was released. I found her the third time, flat on the floor in the hallway. She'd been on her way to class. This time the ambulance came to get her, but the cycle was the same. Soon a long weekend came along, and she got some much needed rest and relaxation. The fainting spells stopped, but her extreme work habits continued until she graduated. Her grades were terrific!

I did not realize how abnormal our sleeping, eating, and studying habits were until I reached college and met people who had done equally well in high school, but managed to get enough sleep, nutrition, and free time. I was shocked. It had all seemed so normal and necessary at my boarding school because there was no standard to compare it to. Everyone stayed up late. We all skipped a few meals or ate unbalanced ones. We all worked long hours and complained about it even more. We all battled endless colds. Everyone was tired. These habits were "normal," and the results were expected. Even the faculty fit many of these categories. These behaviors were accepted in this total environment. There was no one to tell us there were other ways. Instead, we lived closely together and rewarded each other for following the norms. This attention reinforced the behavior, eventually creating a spiral of competitiveness, self-pity, sickness, and exhaustion. We paid our dues.

12

Partying

by Ivan Holmes

I attended a backwards, behind-the-times junior high school before going to boarding school. Yes, I had been stoned before, and even drunk a few times, but it wasn't what we did for fun. In my estimation, I came from a pretty wholesome town. All my life, I had been more concerned with television, girls, or just goofing off after school than with getting high. When I finally left the small town where I grew up to go to a school where kids my own age had more money and time than they knew what to do with, I was in for quite a surprise.

During my first semester, I remained a relatively naive fourteen-year-old. I was not doing well academically, but it wasn't because of drugs or alcohol. I never really thought that anyone at my school could have been very involved with drugs. They never really interested me. Late one night when I was sitting in the common room of my dorm staring at my homework. I overheard two guys having a conversation. One said to the other: "Hey, man, I'm gonna need some speed tomorrow morning to get me through the day, all right?" His friend simply laughed and remarked that it was no problem; he had plenty. As I sat there, I didn't know what to feel. I guess it struck me that I didn't know as much as I thought about what was going on at the school.

It was not until late spring of my first year that I began to take part in the "craziness." At this point, I had made friends with a lot of upperclassmen and was hanging out with them more of the time. One morning, I got up early and went to my friend Bill's room. It was a school day, but too early for anyone to be up yet. Bill packed a knapsack with bagels, cream cheese and a bottle of champagne. We were taking breakfast to his girlfriend and her roommate, champagne and orange juice included. We quietly opened the door of one of the girls' dorms. I was excited; my mind was not functioning properly. Here I was, a freshman in a senior girl's room, drinking champagne at seven o'clock in the morning on a school day. The possibility of getting caught never crossed my mind. After our hour long breakfast, Bill helped my drunken body down the steps to classes. I spent the rest of the day in a daze.

Being new at a school where most people already knew each other, I spent a lot of time during my first year establishing close relationships. A large part of getting to know someone at boarding school is being able to give them support and listen to their problems. The relationship between me and my friend Alison is a perfect example. By this time, I had come to the realization that there were a lot of drugs at school, but the magnitude of the problem had not yet hit me. Then I encountered the first person who had a serious problem. On many occasions, I would skip study hall in order to help Alison sort out her concerns. We would go to the local fast-food restaurant, and I would listen to her drone on in a shaky voice about the drugs she took every day in order to function in a "normal" way. Over the few months I did this, I watched her health deteriorate and her state of mind begin to change. I would often see thin scabbed cuts on her wrists and arms from the past week's flirtations with suicide. It scared me to see my friend this way, but I was not about to turn her over to get medical help. Maybe I should have, but at the time, I was an impressionable freshman. I listened closely to the upperclassmen who let me know it was not cool to rat on your friends.

Regardless of the fact that I had seen the problem that drugs could present, I started using them during my sophomore year. I began to enjoy smoking pot. Bill did it a lot, and I soon fell into the pattern of doing it more than once a week. I had been drinking more and more, and it was fun, but pot was great.

Parties I had never seen before began popping up all over the place. A group of my friends and I went into the city one Saturday, so we could get stoned and go see a movie. While walking through the streets, we met up with some other friends from school. One of them said he had a "fifty bag," and that we should go smoke it. Minutes later, we entered a friend's apartment. She informed us her mom would be back in three hours and to try and be careful.

I can't even remember who was at that party, except that somebody brought a lot of pot and liquor. The party is just a blur in my memory because of the drugs and alcohol I consumed. I almost blacked out, in a sense. One minute I was sitting on the floor of this girl's apartment, and the next, I was lying in the back seat of a small car on my way back to school. The guy driving was a student who had previously graduated from our school. He was just as stoned and drunk as I. I was hastily escorted up to my room where I washed my face, brushed my teeth (to cover up any lingering scents), and got into bed. I was too out of it to worry about an encounter with my dorm proctor.

Pot and alcohol had become familiar to me by this time, and I was having fun with them. The students I hung around with were mostly upperclassmen. Because of this, they had already moved on to other stimulants. Seeing these friends doing cocaine, mushrooms, LSD, and other more serious drugs was unsettling. Drugs of this sort were new and scary to me, and it was difficult to stay away from them, but luckily, I did. My companions knew I was against them, so did not push me to experiment. This was one aspect of boarding school I found reassuring. Peer pressure for me in the boarding atmosphere was minimal. The drugs were there, and one could find them if one wanted to. I cannot remember a time when a friend or anyone pressured me against my will. This lack of peer pressure, at least in my experience, benefitted the community in two ways. First, it kept those, who did no drugs on their own, drug free. Second, for those who were using drugs, the only ones to blame for any problem which arose were themselves.

At the end of tenth grade, I think I had finally graduated to a full user. It was then that I first began to buy my own pot. My roommate and I bought about an eighth between us. We split the $ 25.00 cost and always got stoned together. It became almost a game to sneak around behind the teachers' backs in order to get stoned. At first, avoidance was essential. When I gained the ability to control myself while influenced, I started to get a little braver.

There were various places around town students would frequent without the fear of getting busted. All were quite out of the way, but within easy walking distance. One Friday afternoon, my roommate and I decided to visit our favorite smoking locale. We rode our bikes into the depths of the town graveyard and chose a secluded spot in which to light up. We filled the pipe's bowl, carefully, so none would go to waste, and got stoned. Five bowls later, I realized I could not even focus on the surrounding trees. My head was spinning. We were laughing so hard it hurt. All control was lost; never before had I been this stoned. I do not know how long it was before we finally pulled ourselves together. Some hysterical moments later, we managed to weave our way out of the graveyard.

Riding my bike back to campus, I thought I was going to die. My line of vision was only about three feet long, and I felt like I was the only one on the road moving. Fortunately, I was able to steer clear of cars, and we made it back unharmed. I suddenly realized I was meant to run the Friday night movie in the auditorium and had failed to pick up the film at the student activities office. My first thought was to forget it; I really didn't want to deal with it. Instead, I convinced myself I would have no problem and went to see the director in charge. She didn't seem to notice that I was baked out of my mind, and only mentioned that I looked really tired. Unable to help me acquire the movie, she referred me to security, who would open up the office for me. I explained my problem to the offensive fat man from security, and he suggested we go get the director who had the key. I found myself walking, stoned beyond belief, between two of the school's most tyrannical faculty members. Although I was convinced I was as good as expelled, neither of them noticed. The few moments I was with them lasted forever, but I came out on top, safe and stoned.

By junior year, my friends and I had lost all sense of reality when it came to partying. As I have said, we started our "career" with a cautious attitude.

The fear of expulsion was so great that we took extensive precautions so as to avoid an accident. At first, the majority of our drinking/pot smoking occurred off campus. As our bravery increased, we dared to occasionally "toke up" in the bathroom late at night. Finally, since they had still failed to catch us, we became increasingly blatant in our disregard for the rules.

Drinking often took place in the room as early as eleven-thirty right after final check-in. We would venture to the bathrooms or onto the roof, bong or joint in hand, by midnight. One Saturday night, a group of us invaded an empty room on the third floor. It was only midnight, but a case of beer and a hefty bag of pot were produced. Fans were set up by the windows in order to minimize the amount of smoke. Regardless of all the precautions taken, the entire third floor reeked of marijuana and Budweiser. Again, we were all too blitzed to worry much about the faculty member who lived just below and whose door remained open long after the party began. This is merely one example of how my friends and I were beginning to live a little more dangerously. At the time, I felt like we were breaking all the rules, but as I later found out, much more could be done.

Homework was out of the question once the dorms were locked for the night. Only when the majority of us had work would anything get done. Most of the time we spent our nights screwing around in each others' rooms until long after the official "lights-out" time. There was always something to drink or smoke somewhere in the dorm once the house parents were asleep. One would assume that living in such an atmosphere would put a damper on what we learned, but if you were smart, you got your studying done before curfew or on the weekends, when there was more time to be apart from the crowd.

When I look back, I am amazed at how much I actually did learn, although I spent a lot of time getting wasted and blowing off my homework. This amazement probably comes from the fact that the more-fun times seem to stick in my mind rather than the times devoted to studying. Parties came in shifts. I would spend a week or two partying every night, drinking into the wee hours of the morning. But then a period would come when none of us would really feel like getting drunk, or else we didn't have any liquor. At the very least, we had some conscience about how much work we were or weren't getting done. My friends and I were juniors, which made us very concerned about which college we would go to. We knew that if we let our grades go down too far, it would be impossible to get into the college of our choice. It is important to realize that though we did have fun and party a lot, we were as responsible as necessary in order to succeed in class.

It was eleven o'clock the night before dorm rotation. The next day we would switch roommates, and I would become one of three student dorm heads for the spring term. The move I had to make was small, only from the third to the first floor in the same dorm. The faculty herded us into the dorms after dinner, and we proceeded to pack up our belongings and get ready to move the next day. At around eleven o'clock, my roommate-to-be came into my room with a big grin on his face. "You guys wanna get stoned?" he asked, waving a hefty bag of reefer in front of our noses.

"Later. We have to finish packing," I answered. "How about at around one we all go up onto the roof?" He agreed and the plans were made. But he couldn't wait for one o'clock so ended up doing bong hits by himself in the third floor bathroom. When we finally finished packing at about one-thirty, he again appeared. I asked him if he still wanted to smoke; he said he was game, so he, my roommate, and I proceeded to crawl out on the roof. There was still a thick layer of ice over most of it. My new roommate, in his stoned state of mind, lost his footing and began to slide down the incline. As he slid, the ice broke off in large chunks and noisily fell to the ground, crashing on the pavement. Fortunately, he caught himself on a chimney and safely got inside.

While on the roof, we had made quite a discovery. We had found a full case of beer cooling above the bathroom. We left it there for the time being and went into the bathroom to smoke some weed. After about ten or so bong hits, we were so gone we forgot about the beer. Soon, the munchies set in, and the three of us headed downstairs in search of food. It was three-thirty when a friend of mine came into the room and said someone had stolen his beer. We were still stoned out of our minds even though we had been munching on chips and cookies for an hour or so. After about five minutes of hysterical laughter, we told him we had found it on the roof, but had left it there. We finally retrieved the beer and inhaled it into our already intoxicated bodies. By about five-thirty, I could hardly move. All the beer and food were gone and the party was over, so I went to bed. A mere three hours later, I was awakened by the dorm faculty member, who asked me to get up so I, as dorm proctor, could help her with dorm rotation. There I was, at eight-thirty in the morning, staring red-eyed into the face of the most powerful of all the house parents on campus, and I was still stoned. What a nightmare that was.

That spring was the first time I had switched roommates. I did this because I thought I needed time away from my roommate of two years. We weren't getting along as well as we had been. This was a mistake; my new roommate had a lot of problems. He was a new sophomore and was having difficulty dealing with the freedom and lack of parental supervision. He was starting to really get into pot and was having a hard time going more than a day without it. Soon he was getting stoned every day and, by the time we moved in together, often more than once a day. At first, I got stoned a lot with him, but I eventually got sick of pot and stayed straight most of the time. Our room was on the first floor right next to two bathrooms. Every night, he lit up in one of the johns, either with a friend or alone with his bong. Grass got to be so important to him, he spent most of his money on it and, as he told me later, basically an entire day traveling on public transportation to buy his supply.

I tried many times to talk to him, to tell him he had a problem with pot, but he never wanted to listen. A couple of times, though, he did tell me he wanted to quit and even gave me his marijuana with instructions not to give it back. Sure enough, within a day or so, he would ask for it back. Unfortunately for him, I had usually smoked it all by then and could give him nothing.

The end of my junior year was the first time I tried harder drugs. The drugs were not that much more serious than alcohol or grass, but they were pills, and it was weird to do something like this. Valium was the first pill I ever took, and I liked it a lot. My friend gave me ten of these little white pills, which all had the number "2" on them. The number indicated the milligrams. My friend said that five of them would get me off; I took five and gave five away. At first, I just sat in front of the T.V. and didn't think anything was happening. As time passed, I began to feel sort of tired and got up to go to bed. When I stood up, my legs gave out and I went crashing to the floor. Jesus Christ was I wasted! My whole body was so relaxed that I didn't care where I was or what I was doing; everything was comfortable. At about five in the morning, I got into my bed and slept until late the next day. When I finally did get up on Sunday afternoon, I was so mind-dead that I felt like I was walking through warm jello the rest of the day.

The second experience I had with Valium was quite unpleasant. Two of my pals and I drove up to Vermont one weekend to visit some friends at UVM. On the way, two of us, not the driver, took five milligrams of Valium each, followed by numerous shots of Jack Daniels. Little did we know this can be a deadly combination. Luckily, neither of us had taken a fatal amount, but my friend passed out in the back of the car.

By the time we arrived in Burlington, it was past five in the morning. The other passenger and I were burnt out at this point and only wanted to go to bed. But the driver had remained sober throughout the trip and was itching to drink. Fortunately our host had stocked up on beer. After our driver drank the rest of the night away, we awoke to visit my friend's sister, who lived in downtown Burlington. While we sat around the living room of her apartment, she asked if we wanted to get high. A substantial amount of pot was produced, and we proceeded to do about five hours' of bong hits. The room was spinning for me. We had emptied the cupboards of all the food. What I remember the most from that day was sitting in front of the T.V. with my arms and legs twitching and writhing out of control, trying to figure out what the show was exactly about. I don't think I have been more stoned than I was that night. I didn't even know where I was or what day it was.

Senior year eventually rolled around. The fall semester was the worst of our lives. We were supposed to do two things: keep our grades up and/or bring them up, and visit, interview, and apply to a variety of colleges. Every day was spent with a stomach ache, knowing we could and should be working harder. Feelings of regret ate away at our brains; maybe if we had studied more, we would have done better and our college list would have been more impressive. Almost every conversation was about grade averages, SAT scores, interviews, college essays, and on and on. It seemed like our lives were at an end, for we were now faced with the unavoidable future. Parties were reserved for the weekends. Even then, the whole weekend was spent worrying about the week to come and the work that had to be done.

When looking back at this first semester of my senior year, only a few stories come to mind. All were kind of unpleasant because of the stress I was under. One Friday night, I got stoned with a few friends. It was only about a half hour before curfew, and I was really stoned. Back in the dorm, I began to feel sick as hell and thought I was going to throw up. I was petrified because the resident proctor was still up and around. If I were to get busted, it would be the end of life as I knew it. I could hold my stomach no more. I ran to the bathroom, and in order to cover the sounds of vomiting, I turned on the shower and lost my cookies in the toilet. My house parent did come in and see me throwing up. If she found out that I was stoned, I could be expelled! I used all my strength to put on a normal face and told her I had been in bed all afternoon with stomach flu. She fell for it.

In all, I think my senior year was the most out of control of my life, not only for me, but for the other boarders as well. At any time on a spring weekend night the campus was alive with activity. People were constantly running in and out of the dorms far after in-dorm time. All of us had blatant disregard for the rules. It often seemed like the school was just a bunch of alcoholics. I was no better than anyone else, but it was as if we had to get drunk or stoned every weekend night, or else the weekend was a bad one.

One slow Saturday night, my roommate, another friend and I decided to ditch the dorm and drive into Boston. Although it was against the rules, my roommate had a car near campus. The plan was that we would sneak out at one-thirty and drive into the city to meet a friend who was staying at her cousin's apartment. It was the first time I had ever done this, and I was nervous as hell. My heart pounded as I scraped the fire escape door over the ice-covered roof. I only had to run down the steps and across the street, but it looked as if it was a mile away. The only place we had to worry about was the street. It was well lit, and we would be visible to any security guards in the area. The three of us bolted across; we had passed the first test. Now my roommate had to go and retrieve his car. As the two of us waited impatiently, we smoked cigarettes and spoke nervously about what would happen if we got caught. Long minutes passed before we finally heard the noise of the '67 Volvo approaching.

When we got to the city, it was almost two-thirty. We found the cousin's apartment and rang the doorbell. When she answered, she told us to stay quiet; she did not want the neighbors to get annoyed. We tried our hardest to stay under control, but after a few drinks, we lost it. The people downstairs had called twice by now to tell us to shut up, so we decided to leave and walk around the streets for a while. This was a mistake. My roommate pulled a pellet gun out of his coat, and he and our other friend began shooting things along the way. We all started arguing and heaving insults back and forth. By the time we reached the square, nobody was talking. In a drunken stupor, we quietly staggered throughout the cold streets of Cambridge. A half hour later, we headed back to the apartment; still, no one was on speaking terms. Our friend was acting unreasonable and would not come inside. He insisted on sleeping in the car. I tried, but to no avail, to get him to come out of the cold into the cousin's apartment.

The worst part about our ruined night was the fact that we were putting our high school careers on the line. We would not know whether we had been discovered or not until we got back to school the next day. A feeling of uneasiness remained in our stomachs all night. If we were busted, it would be the end. All of us had certainly had very different ideas about what the night was going to be like. Personally, I hadn't really thought about it very much because I was nervous about sneaking out. My friend and my roommate had wanted to let loose and go nuts. Our friend in town, well, I don't know what she had in mind, but it did not include shooting the town full of pellets. It was already seven in the morning, and we decided to go home. Our friend still had not come inside, so we just went out to get in the car with him. Before leaving, I made sure to call a friend in my dorm to find out if the faculty member knew about our escapades. During the car ride back, we all settled our differences. Our friend in town had stayed behind. It was a while later that she finally forgave us, and I don't blame her for getting so bummed. She was most mad at the fact that we drank all her cousin's beer, as she had clearly instructed us not to, but we could not resist. It was not until we had safely entered the dorm when the anxiousness in my stomach let up. This was the first time I had ventured out of the dorm after hours and would not do it again until much later in the year.

Senior spring was indeed a time of no work and an abundance of parties. It was the second semester; these grades would have no effect on the decisions of the colleges. All the applications had been sent out, and we were waiting for the responses. On March 1st, my life changed drastically. I switched dorms again, moving into a house of all seniors. The actual concept of this dorm was quite ridiculous. It was supposed to prepare the graduating class for college by putting them in a coed dorm, giving them less supervision and later hours. What it says to the seniors is: "We don't give a damn what you do, as long as we don't see you do it."

The first night in my new dorm was uneventful. It was, in a way, confusing. A group of us just sat around in a circle looking at each other. "So this is what it's like, huh?" one of my friends interjected. If it was, it was very anticlimactic. All we had done all night was sit around and talk, not much fun at all. So far, everything we had done could be done in underclass dorms. There was nothing to drink, nothing to smoke, not even cigarettes. There wasn't even anything to eat. It was pathetic. There were two senior dorms, and the other one had a big party that first night and made sure to rub it in our faces the next day. They took every chance they could to tell us how much more fun their dorm was than ours. It was at that moment that the competition began.

After awhile, we found it necessary to at least drink something each night, or else we were bored. It was good when March vacation came, for it gave us a while to cool out and put things back in perspective. Upon returning from vacation, all the college acceptance/rejection letters arrived. Everyone was either happy or hysterically sad, and we were all nervous and in touchy moods. The letters became excuses to party, either in celebration or in mourning. That whole week was kind of a depressing blur to me. I had already been rejected from my first choice school over vacation and was in no mood to get more rejections. As soon as I got back to campus, I got other rejection letters in the mail. My health plummeted. Apart from the depression, I was not eating right. I was smoking two packs of cigarettes a day and was drinking a lot. A week later, I had finally gotten into a couple of schools, but was feeling only a little better. That weekend, I, along with two of my friends, went to relax at my home. Relaxing is not exactly what we did. That weekend was the first time I tried LSD. To say the least, the experience was a shock to my system. It was still quite cold out. We took the acid and walked around the beaches for almost nine hours, not once going inside. We enjoyed ourselves that day, in our drugged-out oblivion, but it is something I haven't and do not wish to repeat ever again. Tripping on acid was a bit much for my system and just wasn't worth doing again.

Senior spring was soon really under way. Before we knew it, it was late April, and the lives of the seniors had become completely free. Nobody cared about grades, homework, or classes, as by this time, we had hopefully been accepted at the college of our choice and had nothing to worry about. These days in the late spring of our last year of high school became some of the best times in our lives.

Each night, there was activity in the dorm into the early morning hours. We disregarded all rules and did as we pleased. Although it was not allowed, three students in my dorm had cars near campus, making the nearby liquor stores more accessible. Several times a week, we ventured out to stock up on beer and vodka. Each night, at least one dorm room had numerous people partying. The parties were all-night fiascoes of beer-drinking and pot or cigarette-smoking, as we huddled around an open window. We usually found ourselves frantically stowing the empties and airing out the room at eight in the morning.

One Monday night, which will not only remain in the minds of my dormmates, but also in the school's folklore for years to come, was the keg party. I do not really remember how the idea came about, only that it was a pretty spontaneous thing. As far as we knew, there had never been a keg party on campus before. Money was immediately raised, rather borrowed, from a friend. Then we found the student with the most convincing fake I.D. and went to the liquor store. The quarter-keg was smuggled into the dorm by way of a laundry bag suspiciously stretched over its exterior.

That night, the entire dorm, all twenty of us, gathered in one of the third floor bedrooms. The keg was awkwardly tapped, and the party began. Although we convinced ourselves we were being relatively quiet, there must have been a substantial amount of noise coming from the room. We all desperately hoped the dorm faculty member would not be awakened, as getting caught this late in our high school career would have been catastrophic.

As the party progressed, we became dissatisfied with the surroundings and about sixteen of us ventured out onto the fire escape and up to the roof. We sat up there in near silence at three o'clock drinking flat beer and smoking. It was not long before our peace was rudely disrupted. Below us we heard the security guards talking in loud voices and were sure we had been busted. Clearly, at that juncture, it was beneficial to vacate the roof, as that was a serious offense in itself. Everyone scrambled for the fire escape ladder, and almost everyone managed to get inside without too much noise. Unfortunately, the last person brushed against the cover of the outside light causing it to roll down the roof and shatter outside the house parent's window.

For the next hour, the entire dorm waited in fear of the house parent coming upstairs. We later found out she had been awakened, but had decided to trust us and not check up on our activities. Even so, it was quite clear to the rest of the campus that something had gone on that night. The following day at eight in the morning, we all filed out of the dorm looking hungover and exhausted. The question still remains of how much the other students and faculty actually knew.

By the time graduation week rolled around, we were ready to leave our home of several years. Of course, we were saddened by the prospect of leaving loved friends, but not the school itself. The day before graduation involved cleaning and packing. To both my roommate's and my dismay, we had quite a task before us. Out of laziness, we had neglected to dispose of three months' worth of beer cans and liquor bottles. We realized we had over two-hundred empties in our room and no way to dispose of them. Instead of merely sneaking them out to the garbage, we insisted on being brash. We put the returnables into trash bags and carried them downtown to the liquor store. With the deposit money, we purchased a large bottle of vodka for that night's festivities.

The party extended throughout the campus. There were few, if any, students who slept that night. Just by glancing out the window, one saw students of all ages running between the dorms. The senior dorms were packed with underclassmen sitting in the hallways drinking beer and smoking cigarettes.

The dorm was so loud, I am still amazed we weren't caught by either a faculty member or security. The entire place was up all night partying together for the last time. Before we knew it, graduation was over, and we were just beginning to sober up.

In reading the stories and memories accounted for here, it is necessary to keep things in perspective. By no means do I intend to present my alma mater or my experience at the school as one big, drug-crazed party. Attending a private boarding school opened many valuable doors for me, both socially and educationally. Those years were the richest I have had thus far. They enabled me to learn to communicate and interact with people in such a way that would have been difficult in a different setting. My appreciation of education and knowledge has increased one-hundredfold. Partying was merely one aspect of boarding school I am thankful to have experienced. I was able to sow many of my proverbial oats before entering college, which now allows me to concentrate on my studies perhaps more than I would have otherwise.

13

S'wonderful

by Dan Peters

One of the things that amazed me most after leaving prep school was learning that not everyone thought of their time there as fondly as I did. For me, there is no debate: my prep school was the most profoundly valuable experience I have ever had. This sounds like just another cliched, trite reminiscence of a preppie yearning for his "wonderful years," but the truth is that I developed more of the principles I now hold dear and initiated more lifelong friendships in those four years than at any other point in my fairly young life. For several of my friends and me, my school was the decisive factor in our education and in the development of our personalities. On more than one occasion, I have heard a classmate say that college was simply a four-year transition between prep school and the real world. The obvious question, then, is what in the world was so wonderful about it? Even more importantly, what was it about my prep school that I found so wonderful that so many of my classmates found barely tolerable?

My fondness for my prep school is traceable to three central elements: the sheer wealth of activities and opportunities that not only kept me happily occupied through four long New England winters, but also challenged me intellectually and physically; the care and personal attention of a varied faculty that knew when to act as policemen and when to act as friends and confidants; and most importantly, a caliber and variety of friends which I will keep for a lifetime.

In general terms, the school's philosophy was that students will stay happy and out of trouble if they stay busy. The result was an abundance of extracurricular activities appealing to every possible interest, as well as mandatory chapel, seated dinner attendance several times a week, and requisite hours for dorm check-in. There was also a sports requirement for the lower classes, and of course our daily class schedule. But beyond these minimal guidelines, our days were our own. Personally, I was all too happy to oblige the school with my extracurricular participation. In all my four years, there was rarely a time that I was not playing a sport, singing, acting, deejaying for the radio station, and working on the newspaper — all simultaneously. I lived with a roommate two out of four years (although only once voluntarily), and had a serious girlfriend for three. Perhaps it was the fact that we were in a rural area, but for some reason it seemed perfectly natural to be involved in two dozen activities. To be honest, I must point out that my initial naivete and shyness welcomed a busy schedule to keep me occupied and my thoughts away from home. Stronger or more independent personalities among my classmates may have gotten frustrated by even the school's few regulatory guidelines. What may have seemed like a reasonable hour to me to be confined to my dorm — ten at night on weekdays and eleven on Saturdays — may have appeared an unreasonable or unnecessary burden to others. By my senior year, I also felt that these guidelines were a bit immature, but my "responsible" side didn't want to face the wrath of the faculty or my parents if I chose to ignore them. Besides, with all my activities, a bed was always a welcome conclusion to the day.

In considering those who took advantage of the abundant opportunities at prep school, it struck me that there was probably a type of person who thrived best in that environment. Social circles at my school drew serious lines of demarcation, so for the meek and shy it was probably a difficult place to survive. I have known friends who have said the school was a lonely place — that they "floated" through their years without any emotional ties to anyone — and all I can think is that I was far too immersed to notice. My older sister preceded me at the same school. As a result, I "inherited" a group of friends that she left behind and so never truly had to struggle to find a welcoming group of peers. I will also give myself some credit in saying that the group changed, as we all changed in our years there, to reflect more of who I was and less of who my sister had been. Even so, guiding a ship is much easier when one is on board.

Personalities in the opposite extreme probably also fared uncomfortably. If you arrived at the school with immature confidence and a touch of independence, the faculty was quick to recognize your potential. If you took these traits one step further, to arrogance and rebelliousness, the school truly became a claustrophobic community. Faculty and students alike were always looking over your shoulder, and the only option for total privacy was covert action. It was only a matter of time before you were discovered.

Each of us is a natural victim of our own upbringing. In my case, I had the sheer luck of entering prep school when I was as moldable as a brick of clay, and meeting peers and professors alike whose principles were worthy of my admiration. As the years passed and I was cogent of my own direction, I realized my parents had instilled in me the desire to face certain challenges and accept certain responsibilities. In all, my prep school offered opportunities. Whether you were intelligent or mature enough to recognize their value, or whether you had the fortune to be guided by those who were, is a question that was decided long before you arrived at the school.

What my prep school had, in addition to all these opportunities, was a faculty that cared. I don't mean simply a faculty that was brilliant in the classroom and receptive to insightful questions, but also a group of teachers whom you could look upon as friends. My junior year, I lived next door to a junior faculty member who always left his door open. On more than one occasion I would drop by just to chat. On Saturday nights when he was on duty, the joke was to come in with your best dramatic performance of a stumbling drunk. I'm sure many parents and educators would be shocked that I could even joke about such a serious infraction, but the point is that this faculty member wouldn't hesitate to "bust" you if he found you drinking. As long as it was a prank, he was human enough to be your friend and share your humor. This one faculty member was also human enough to share with you some of the details of the faculty gossip — an otherwise sacrosanct topic. Certainly one of the reasons he was this casual was his age, but there were more senior faculty members who also revealed their humanity.

My senior year, my friend and I lived together in a dorm run by one of the most idolized teachers at the school. Early in the year, he made it very clear that he was our friend, teacher and advisor, UP TO A POINT! If he caught us breaking the rules, he would first turn us in, and then play our advocate in the disciplinary meeting to follow. Needless to say, my roommate and I were sufficiently in awe of this man that we decided not to test his word. We became great friends with him, and over the course of the year had hilarious conversations on every topic under the sun. (He was also one of the wittiest teachers at school.) Somewhere along the line my roommate and I managed to convince him, tongue-in-cheek, that we were transvestite lovers. The topic always brought a laugh. Finally, the night before Christmas break, my roommate and I concocted a plan. A year earlier he had played a drag queen in a school talent show and still had the makings of a costume. As he prepared the scene, I went to tell our favorite dormmaster that we had a Christmas present for him in our room.

As he opened the door, it was dark except for the pink glow of Christmas lights in one corner. There, on our couch, my roommate was lounging in fishnet stockings and a leather vest, playing his clarinet with a "come hither" look in his eyes. Our teacher friend let loose with the most concerned "OH MY GOD" I have ever heard, and my roommate and I exploded in roars of laughter. Given the stories I have heard of some high school professors, I think it's fair to say our relationship with him was very good.

In addition to this closeness outside the classroom, the sheer number of teachers at the school allowed for personal attention inside the classroom as well. My senior year, I had not one, but two tutorials with professors in which I was one of only two students. In one case, I studied Italian, a language not normally offered at my school. In the other, I had the opportunity to pursue a psychology tutorial with a teacher who , to this day, remains a close personal friend. In fact, our forty minute sessions spent discussing everything from Jung and Freud to parapsychology and meditation, often lapsed into hour-and-a-half long dialogues on the nature of conscientious objection and peaceful resistance. Teachers at my school welcomed the opportunity to expand our horizons, and if that meant pursuing issues of the students' own choice that were not on any normal curriculum, then they were usually all too happy to adjust their own schedules to make time. Perhaps one of the key factors that led to such a close bond between students and faculty was the fact that faculty were required to take on a number of roles. They were not only teachers in the traditional classroom sense, but also shared with you the victories of sport as your coach, the trials and tribulations of management as your newspaper or radio station advisor, and the joys of life and love as your dormitory master. There was no escaping them if you wanted to, but more accurately, there was rarely any reason to want to.

The essential grace of the faculty can be distilled to one simple observa-tion: they provided students with the perfect balance of freedom and support. For those students who chose to live their lives without typical parental supervision, the faculty were generally happy to act as teachers and coaches and little more. On the other hand, the faculty were also eminently approach-able, and the slightest call for help usually resulted in a wave of concern. Given the nature of a school set in the country, the faculty were also welcome to simply be our friends. Particularly those faculty members without family must have felt isolated at my school, and it doesn't take a psychologist to note that even friendly discussion with a teenager can alleviate the ultimate bore-dom of a long winter. Looking back, I realize that all it really took to under-stand the faculty was to realize that they were also human.

In a community in which sharing was so important — sharing your intel-lectual ideas with your classmates, sharing your personal hopes and fears with your friends, and often sharing some combination of the two with your teach-ers, advisors, and coaches — students who felt antagonistic to the faculty often missed one of the dearest parts of the school. The faculty were always quick to respect you as a young adult, and this was one of the reasons for the resulting camaraderie on campus. Those students who chose to ignore the guidelines of the school, to the extent that they were always cautious about their connection with the faculty, lost the spark that made day-to-day living such a pleasant event. In succinct terms, the only time that student-faculty relations were reduced to "us" and "them" were when they were forced that way by a student. The faculty generally gave us every benefit of the doubt.

For whatever reason it is in life that one makes friends, something about my school made it the perfect breeding ground for friendships. In a class of more than 100 students, one is bound to make acquaintances, but somehow

I managed to elevate a lot of relationships to the status of lifelong friends. Recently, on an average Saturday night in New York City, I ran into six classmates who were going out together to a club, roughly a decade after we had graduated. On another occasion, I ran into eight classmates enjoying an evening drink. And I personally spend every Thanksgiving with at least four classmates, year after year, regardless of our private or professional lives. I have been in two classmates' weddings, and expect most of my own ushers to be prep school classmates.

As I was going through prep school, I increasingly realized that I was experiencing something unique. My junior year, my parents made one comment that still sticks in my mind: "People don't usually have more than one, or at most two best friends, but you seem to have five or six." Indeed, for whatever reason, I was blessed with the chance to meet six people with whom I shared so much in common. We went on to live together, work together, play and struggle and rejoice together during four years at prep school. Each of us went to different universities, and as a testament to my prep school, with only one exception, we are all still close friends. In terms of a valid argument for going to a particular school, one can hardly entice candidates by promising that they will make friends. On the other hand, I look back on my prep school and realize my friends are my most cherished product of those years.

My school did a great job of respecting and fostering friendships. With the exception of my freshman year (when my roommate, and actually my entire dorm, was a disaster), I roomed next to a close friend every year. Beyond that, my entire group of friends, even as it changed, managed to live near one another year after year. The school must have had a superb social sense to realize exactly where social alliances were formed.

My school was always known as having extremely relaxed rules for "intervisitation" — the prep school term for visiting dorms of the opposite sex. For two hours every afternoon and three or more every night, boys and girls were allowed to visit each other in their rooms. There were no "open door" rules, no "three feet on the floor," but simple privacy. The benefit of this was intensified relationships between the sexes. I don't just mean more people were sleeping together (which is probably true but not my point), but more boys and girls were actually becoming close platonic friends. When I finally reached college, it seemed so amazing to me that so many of my peers had not had this essential experience. Once again, it was the trust of the school leaders in the maturity of the students that led to increased personal responsibility and, eventually, the development of our own maturity.

My prep school was certainly a number of different things to different people. The luxury of being able to take part in a variety of extracurriculars (which becomes impossible once you hit college because of time commitments) both broadened your horizons and forced you to meet people under a variety of circumstances. With everything going on, it was probably possible for the meek to get "lost in the wash," but it probably also proved to be an important lesson in preparation for college. (That is, after all, what a "prep school" is supposed to be.) For everyone, prep school meant chapel and seated dinner several days a week. It meant a particular class junior year that taught the religious philosophy of Paul Tillich. It was hockey games and crew races, field hockey and lacrosse. The radio station had a huge following, while the newspaper had an insanely devoted core group. There was ballet and drama and three different singing groups. The extroverts among us could attempt to do it all, while those who were timid could choose their single favorite. Every spring, crew jocks flocked around the varsity coach like apostles, hovering over every word. Some faculty members had little tea parties with favorite students, while others preferred to grab an entire dorm and go out for ice cream. It was all there.

My prep school was not, as I reflect upon it after four years of college, particularly liberal or tolerant. No one "came out of the closet." There were only a handful of Jewish students and a handful of African Americans. My school was set in its ways, and I understand it is getting worse rather than better. Only after I graduated did I hear of the widespread use of drugs — somehow I never witnessed it while I was there. I guess in some ways that's good — there was never any peer pressure. But I hear that the new headmaster is clamping down on all regulations. (I worry about what that might do to the communal sense of trust). Still, my school managed to endow me with ideals necessary for civilized living: honesty, integrity, perseverance, joie de vivre. Whether this was nature or nurture is beyond my ability to determine.

I came out of my prep school with the skills necessary to communicate eloquently, a group of friends I will have for life, and a set of principles I can be proud of. For these, I can only be thankful.

14

A Fine Line: Student-Faculty Intimacy

by Tanya Last

On today's episode of "The Brady Bunch," Greg is flunking math. His teacher is a leggy young woman in a minidress. As she bends over Greg's desk, her long auburn hair, sprayed into a stiffened flip, brushes his shoulder. She defines the term "hypotenuse."

We've all had crushes on our teachers — it's part of growing up. The syndrome is a familiar, even forgivable, one. At the tail end of the episode (right before the upbeat reprise of the theme song), Mr. Brady admits to Greg's teacher: "If I had a teacher who looked like you, I'd have been flunking math, too."

But what if Greg's math teacher, instead of reiterating her geometry lesson, had flung away the math book and unzipped Greg's fly? One episode of "The Brady Bunch" would never have made prime time.

What begins as a crush as harmless as Greg's, can develop into a great deal more. Especially at boarding schools, where students and teachers share dining halls and dormitories as well as classrooms, the fine line between friendship and intimacy grows increasingly blurry.

During my first job teaching prep school, I worked as an intern with Nick Kendall. Nick was a member of the English department. His favorite books were *The Great Gatsby*, *The Catcher in the Rye*, and *One Flew Over the Cuckoo's Nest*. Nick was a nice guy, easy to work with, and he had a good rapport with the students. He also had a great set of pecs.

Nick turned Ultimate Frisbee into a spectator sport. One rainy afternoon, a group of teachers decided to have a game — the ultimate joy was sloshing and sliding around as much as possible. To allow the members of each team to tell each other apart, one team wore shirts and the other didn't.

Nick was a No-shirt. Within fifteen minutes, the game had drawn quite a crowd of onlookers, most of them teenage girls. They nudged each other and widened their blue-smeared eyes when Nick made a dive for the disk; they wailed and giggled when he fell on his rump in the mud.

I proctored a dorm of tenth-grade girls. Sometimes Nick came over to prepare lessons. Before he came over, the girls put on Benetton skirts and leggings, outfits they wore to Saturday night dances. They asked my advice about makeup.

At first, I was merely amused by the furor. After all, a little adulation was to be expected from teenage girls who were presented with an authority figure as young and attractive as Nick Kendall. Besides, a crush was a natural way to release tension in the high-powered atmosphere of a competitive prep school.

As Nick and I wrote up the questions for a Hemingway quiz, I did my best to ignore the excited gasps and whispers we could hear in the corridor. When he left, a swarm of fifteen-year-olds flew into my room.

"I swear, Mr. Kendall is such a fox!"

"Marissa gets to be in one of his classes. She's totally in love with him."

"I'm in love with him, too. Totally."

They asked me how old he was, if he was married. When I finally told them he had a serious girlfriend, some were discouraged. Others told themselves he secretly liked them. They had seen signals.

"I talked to him in the dining hall the other day," boasted Tierney, an athletic blonde. "He said, 'Hi.' We were at the soda machine. He was getting a glass of Coke, and I was getting some Diet Coke, so our hands were right next to each other. They almost touched."

I assumed that Nick was used to such attention, that he took it in stride. He even seemed oblivious to it much of the time. But, eventually, I learned this was not the case. A teenager's lighthearted fantasies could turn into a serious fixation, the bubbly gossip into rumors of sexual harassment.

Nick told me about female students who had flirted with him, asked him on dates, even openly propositioned him. Most of them were older students, juniors or seniors who projected know-how and sophistication.

"They'd catch you completely off guard," Nick told me. "Can you imagine a student who comes to you after class, looks you straight in the eye, and asks you to sleep with her? You don't know how to react."

"And some of these girls really knew how to make themselves attractive. They wore a lot of makeup and dressed very provocatively. It was intimidating. Sometimes I felt that it was me who was the inexperienced one."

Student-faculty relationships take on a variety of possible scenarios. In the most glaring cases of sexual harassment, the teacher will take deliberate advantage of the student, using his or her authority and seeming infallibility to intimidate and gain sexual favors.

Lisa was on a scholarship and needed a B average to graduate. She had trouble with science, however, and her recent biology grades had been in the low C range. Her parents and academic advisor were putting a great deal of pressure on her to improve. Finally, Lisa asked her biology teacher for extra help.

Her teacher readily agreed. Lisa could come to his room twice a week, he told her. In no time, she'd be getting high B's and even A's. Unfortunately, Lisa had to do more than study.

Sexual harassment of this kind is similar to blackmail. If Lisa were to resist her teacher's advances, he might have dropped her grade. If she had reported him, it would only be her word against his. Often, too, the student is unwilling to accuse a figure of authority whose role is not merely educational, but, in a boarding school, parental as well.

On the other side of the situation, the student may falsely accuse a teacher of inappropriate conduct. Sometimes the accusation is based on a misunderstanding.

A resident advisor named Andrew interacted on an openly physical level with the kids in his dorm; he liked to give a student a pat on the back along with a word of advice. Late one night, he found Jane studying at her desk. She jumped, startled; she was supposed to be in bed three hours ago. Andrew told her it was way past curfew. Nervously, Jane explained that tomorrow she was taking the famous killer exam in European history, and she was sure she would flunk it. Assuring Jane she would do just fine, Andrew put his arm around her. Jane tensed up, frightened.

At lunch the next day, Jane seemed touchy and withdrawn. Finally, she confided to a friend that the previous night, while everyone was asleep, her hall proctor had come on to her.

The rumor spread through the dorm. Finally, it came back to Andrew. He sat Jane down for a talk, explaining that he had no intention of seducing her. Jane realized that she had overreacted to Andrew's behavior and apologized. The matter was cleared up, but ever since, Andrew has been scrupulously formal with his students.

Occasionally, however, a student reacts from spite over academic or romantic rejection, and, as revenge, deliberately misrepresents the situation. Although Nick Kendall never accepted any proposition, he was aware of the nasty aftertaste that such a confrontation could leave. Suspicion would be likely to fall on Nick who, as an authority figure and a male, would be assumed to be the more likely aggressor in a case of sexual harassment.

Mr. Crain, a respected history teacher, summoned Mary after a test; he had noticed she was cheating. Mary was already on disciplinary probation, and the punishment for this offense could be expulsion. But Mary found a way to turn the tables on Mr. Crain. She accused him of sexual harassment. Although Mr. Crain eventually won the case, his reputation, hitherto flawless, was irreparably damaged. The following year, he took a job at another school.

Student-faculty dating, however, is not always such a nefarious phenomenon. Not all relationships are tainted by deceit and power games. Many affairs develop from initially innocent and well-meaning friendships.

In the student's eyes, a teacher is a highly attractive figure — older, wiser, and definitely off-limits. The dramatic and performatory nature of the teacher's role encourages students to idolize a faculty member the way they might a movie or rock star.

At the same time, students relish the moments when authority slips. There is nothing more exciting than finding out that your teacher, so remote, so distant, and always so much in control, is just a regular person after all. If given the opportunity, students will ask a teacher all sorts of personal questions, ranging from the superficial to the private. What is your favorite T.V. show? How good were your grades in school? How many brothers and sisters do you have? Were you ever married? Are you going out with somebody now? Who?

For the teacher's part, it is tempting to slip into the student mode. This is especially true of the younger teachers, who have recently finished college, and who may be no more than four or five years older than the seniors they teach.

I was twenty-two when I started teaching, but in shorts and a T-shirt, I looked sixteen. Even fellow teachers mistook me for a student and sometimes would yell at me when they saw me wandering outside my dorm after curfew. I felt I needed to create a professional persona for myself. In class, I cultivated my "schoolmarm look." I wore a straight black skirt, horn-rimmed glasses, and I fastened my hair in a severe knot. My lectures on Jane Austen were precise and formal, delivered with impeccable pronunciation.

One evening after dinner, I was persuaded to join a game of touch football. My students were shocked and delighted. Their prissy English teacher, who was such a hard grader, who paced before the class in black pumps, who punctuated her sentences by tapping the blackboard with a piece of chalk, had been transformed into a rough-and-tumble tomboy. In grass-stained sweats, I barrelled into Mr. Rycroft, the head of the Classics department, and tried to wrench the ball away from him. I could hear some of my shriller students cheering lustily. I have to admit, my heart thrilled at the feeling of popularity, of camaraderie.

In class the next day, my students started ribbing me about the game. Feebly, I proposed that we all get back to *Pride and Prejudice*, but the truth was, I was enjoying myself. I didn't want to talk about the Bennets at Longbourne any more than they did. We wasted ten minutes guffawing. After class, I saw one boy nudge another. "Miss Rich is hot," he whispered.

Student-teacher attraction involves role-reversal. Students project their desires onto their teachers: my image changed from prim and proper to "hot." In the same way, teachers project their desires onto their students; it is in their students that teachers see themselves reflected. It is all too easy to remember what it felt like to be sixteen. A friend once described a student as "really shy and quiet, but pretty in an unconventional way — big blue eyes and a great smile. I don't know why the guys don't notice her. She'd be my type if I were her age."

Remarks like this are made frequently; they are usually harmless and inconsequential. At other times, however, they are the first signs of serious romantic interest, and they should be a red flag.

Belinda Cameron was a friend of mine in the English department, young and spunky with long blonde hair and white sneakers — a "fun teacher," according to her students. One night, as we sat in the dining hall, Belinda pointed out Josh Gardner to me.

"That's one great kid," she said.

Josh was a tall, sturdy boy with red-brown hair and a coppery tan. I had heard his name before from other teachers, who had praised him as an honest, mature young man, kind to the younger students.

"He's a hard worker, too," Belinda added. "He's only a junior in AP English, but he's doing better than most of the seniors. And he always has something good to contribute in class."

For the past three years, Belinda had been carrying on a long-distance relationship with a guy from Montreal named Doug. Things between them were pretty tumultuous. Sometimes Belinda wanted to marry him; at others, she swore to me that she would break things off.

As it turned out, however, it was Doug who broke things off. Over Christmas break, Belinda went to Canada for a visit. Upon her arrival, Doug told her that he had been seeing another woman. "A French bitch with ringlets," Belinda spat at me, "With a preposterous hyphenated name that I can't even pronounce. I went back the same afternoon. I'd barely left the airport."

When the winter term began, Belinda was not herself. She stopped running her daily six miles. She overslept, missing breakfast and sometimes arriving late for class.

One morning, Dottie Farley, the head of the English department, came unexpectedly to sit in on Belinda's class. Belinda had barely prepared her lesson the night before. As she presented Kate Chopin's *The Awakening*, her students seemed half asleep. When she asked questions, no one raised a hand.

"I felt as if I were talking into a void. If it hadn't been for Josh, I'd have flopped before the Farley herself," Belinda told me later.

"What did he do?"

"He baled me out is what he did. He started raising his hand, answering my questions. I guess he could tell I was on the spot. Then he started bringing up his own questions: he asked everybody how it would feel to be Edna, the heroine of *The Awakening*, who is stuck being a wife in New Orleans in the 1800's. Everybody started chiming in. The class just took off! I swear I could have kissed him."

More and more often, Belinda raved about Josh. She pointed him out in the dining hall, in the game room, in the gym. He was such a leader, she said; you'd never guess he was only seventeen. He was a great swimmer too — he had the second best record on the school team.

Josh started hanging around after class and talking to Belinda about books; his favorite character was Darl in *As I Lay Dying*. On a couple of occasions, I saw them running together. Josh was sweating profusely, and Belinda was talking to him between gasps.

One evening, Josh came to Belinda's room for extra help. He was writing a paper on *Heart of Darkness*, and he wanted her to approve his outline.

When Belinda came to the door, she was pale and had been crying. She was on the phone to Montreal, she told Josh; could he wait a few minutes?

When Belinda hung up, Josh rose to his feet. "I could go — we could talk about this another time, Miss Cameron," he began.

"That's okay; I'm fine. I just have a little cold," Belinda said. "Let me wash my face and make some tea, and I'll be right with you."

Belinda washed her face, brushed her hair, and put on makeup. She made tea for herself and Josh, and she brought out a tin of her oatmeal raisin cookies. She looked over his outline, and then they watched the Cosby Show together.

Soon after, I detected that something was amiss. Belinda's moods were always on the swing. One moment, she'd be blushing and sputtering with laughter; the next, she'd be pensive and glum. She taught her classes with frenzied energy. Meanwhile, she made an effort not to talk about Doug.

One night when we were both off duty, I proposed we have drinks together. Over a vodka collins, Belinda told me she and Josh were romantically involved.

I was too surprised to phrase a polite question. "How involved? Sleeping together?"

"Well, no. I mean, I don't think I should. I shouldn't be doing any of this, actually." She shook her head. "I'm so shocked at myself. I feel like Mrs. Robinson. I feel guilty all the time — guilty in class, especially. Like I'm being unfair to the other students. Each time I call on Josh, I blush. I don't even hear his answers. I feel funny grading his papers, like I should sign my comments 'Love, Belinda.' But the fact is, he still calls me Miss Cameron!

"It's weird in the dorm, too. I keep on worrying that my proctees will think it's weird that he's always around."

Belinda sighed. "The funny thing is, I really like Josh. He's so mature, so solid and supportive, the way Doug never was. He cheers me up."

I realized Belinda had suffered a bad blow from Doug, that she was lonely and depressed. I knew she needed an ego boost in her personal life. But I doubted that Josh was as mature as Belinda insisted. I'd see him in the dining hall, flipping jello cubes with his dorm buddies while Belinda drank coffee at the faculty table.

"You should really stop," I told her. "You could get into a lot of trouble. You're a good teacher — it's just not worth it."

Belinda made an effort to be discreet. She was careful not to treat Josh in an overly familiar manner when they were in public. But I knew they were still seeing each other, and at night now, too. A couple of times I called Belinda after curfew when I thought she would be alone. Her nervous stammering and evasive remarks made it clear that Josh was there. I would end the phone call as quickly as possible.

Meanwhile, Josh was feeling alienated from his friends. He couldn't tell them where he was going when he went to see Belinda, so he said he was going to the library instead. His friends were beginning to tease him about being a monk. They complained that he didn't hang out with them the way he used to. What was more, Josh didn't ask out other girls. When his pals compared notes about their love lives, he couldn't contribute. A friend even asked Josh if he was "queer."

One night at two in the morning, there was a fire drill in Josh's dorm. Twenty-one boys filed out of the building, yawning and shivering in their pajamas. There were supposed to be twenty-two. Josh was missing.

The proctors checked the dorm; Josh had a single room, and maybe no one had woken him. They found his room empty. The proctor who had done the headcheck at curfew reported that Josh had been in his room at eleven. Where was he now?

Security put out a search, calling each proctor in each dorm. Belinda was woken up at three in the morning. The firm voice on the receiver told her that a boy named Joshua Gardner was missing; could she keep on the lookout for him, please? She hung up in a panic.

She woke Josh, and they prepared a story. Then Belinda let him out of her dorm through the back way.

The next morning, Josh reported to the Dean of Boys. He said that at midnight the night before, he realized he had lost an English paper. He snuck out of his dorm and went to the computer room where he remembered he had left it. When he returned to his dorm, security had double-locked the doors for the night. He had gone back to the computer room and slept there.

When the dean asked Belinda Cameron about the English paper, she confirmed the statement that he had one due. Satisfied that Josh had not spent the night intaking drugs or alcohol or cavorting with members of the opposite sex, the staff put him on probation for violating curfew.

A couple of days later, Belinda and Josh had a long talk. Both decided they should end their relationship. Belinda would go back to her job, and Josh would go back to his friends.

I was relieved to see they had worked things out quite well. Soon after, Josh started dating a freshman. Belinda met an architect with whom she spent the weekends. Josh still occasionally visited Belinda's room but only for extra help and oatmeal cookies.

A student may seem sophisticated and mature, but an adult relationship puts great pressure on a teenager, especially when the relationship must be kept scrupulously secret. Belinda and Josh recognized the potential danger in their involvement, so they ended their relationship before either person was hurt. In other instances, however, commitments become serious to the point of obsession. The relationship, intensified by its illicit nature, grows beyond the couple's control.

Nina Curtin was a senior in Barrow Hall. She was in the school honors society, and she edited the literary magazine. Her father was a linguistics professor at Princeton, and she had grown up on the college campus. She read incessantly and wanted to be a writer.

Nina had always seemed shy and somewhat mousy in high school. Over the past summer, however, she had lived with a family in France. When she returned as a senior, she had blossomed. She had a small but devoted group of friends, and she enjoyed Saturday night dances. Boys had started to notice her, too. Nina wasn't interested in most of them, however; boys her age seemed so immature. Nina wanted someone smart, she told her friends, someone she could talk to and learn from.

Mr. Braverman lived next door to Barrow, in Lyme Hall. He was young; Nina had heard that he had graduated from Harvard only last year. Mr. Braverman taught political science, and he was a proctor for junior boys. He had only been at the school for two months, but he was already a legend.

Nina had heard that Mr. Braverman was a lunatic. Everybody said his classes were non-stop action. He waved his arms, spewing fiery political opinions. When Mr. Braverman asked a question, all hands would shoot up simultaneously. He was popular in Lyme Hall as well. Kids were always dropping into his room, whether they needed help with homework, a roommate dispute, or just wanted to shoot the breeze.

The first time Nina spoke to Mr. Braverman, she was at the snack bar. He was behind her in line. Nina bought a soda.

"Diet Grape Shasta?" Mr. Braverman asked her in horror. "You can swallow that stuff?"

"It's good," she said. "It tastes like grape juice, and it's only fifteen calories a can."

"It leaves a lovely purple moustache, too," he said.

As they walked back to their dorms together, they talked about philosophy. Nina mentioned Nietzsche and Heidegger to show Mr. Braverman she knew who they were. They continued their talk in his dorm. On his door, the boys had put up the sign: CAUTION ON ENTRY − WORLD'S WEIRDEST PROCTOR. His room was so full of books that they had to be piled in stacks on the floor.

The next morning, Nina made a shy confession to her roommates. She told Susanna and Claire that she had a crush on Mr. Braverman. It was terrible.

He was a teacher. She knew she had no chance with him — not in a million years.

Each day, Nina looked for Mr. Braverman in the library, in the dining hall, at the snack bar. Every time she went in or out of her dorm, she shot a hopeful glance at Lyme next door. She looked at his picture in the school facebook. She memorized his phone number.

Nina listened to what people said about Mr. Braverman, and she savored everything she heard. He had been Phi Beta Kappa at Harvard. He played basketball in college, and he was a Celtics freak. When he taught his classes, he'd throw erasers at you if you didn't pay attention. Nina wondered if Mr. Braverman threw erasers at the girls, too. She wondered if he talked to other girls the same way he talked to her.

But he did like to talk to her. They talked in the dining hall and on the steps of Lyme and Barrow. They discussed politics, family dynamics, the morality of modern science. They quarrelled about the value (or lack thereof, Mr. Braverman insisted) of religious faith. Mr. Braverman gave Nina Freud's *The Future of an Illusion* and told her to read it. Nina read it fastidiously, taking notes.

Sam Braverman, meanwhile, was growing confused. He was merely curious about Nina, he had told himself at first, as he was about many of his students and proctees. But he liked to hear her talk, admired the way her mind worked. He thought she was delicate and pretty, with intelligent eyes. He worried about her too; he thought she didn't eat enough or get enough sleep. Some nights, very late, he looked out at her window in Barrow, and the light was still on.

One afternoon, he saw Nina poring over a textbook in the library. When he approached, she perked up, removing her glasses.

"What are you studying?" he whispered.

"Math," she groaned. "I have a horrible calculus test tomorrow. There is no way in the world I can pass it at this point."

"I'm sure you'll pass it. When did you ever not pass anything, Nina?"

"Well, there's no way I can get above a C."

Mr. Braverman chortled. "Wanna make a bet on that?"

"A bet?"

"Yeah. If you get above a C — no, I'll make it easy for you — above a B — then you buy me coffee. If you get a B or below, then I buy you coffee."

Nina's cheeks were pink. "Deal," she said. They shook hands. It was the first time Mr. Braverman had ever touched her.

Nina got a B +, so she took Mr. Braverman out for coffee. He drove them into the nearby town. They ordered carrot cake and talked for three hours. They almost missed curfew.

Nina started coming to Mr. Braverman's dormitory apartment more and more often. He was always delighted to see her. He lent her more articles to read; she made him copies of her stories and poems, which he found surprisingly sensitive and mature. Their discussions were so animated that Mr. Braverman's proctees were sometimes shy about coming in and interrupting. They gave Nina a nickname: they called her "the Proctorwatcher."

Nina and Mr. Braverman were now having coffee together about once a week. One evening, driving back from town, Mr. Braverman turned to her and said:

"You don't talk to people about this, do you? I mean, you and I know it's only coffee, but other people might get the wrong idea."

"I know," said Nina, wisely. "I won't talk."

But when she returned to her room, she fell down on her bed and cried. "He said it was only coffee," she sobbed to Susanna and Claire. "That's all I am to him."

"Come on, Nina, what can you expect?" Claire demanded. "Maybe Mr. Braverman would go out with you if you didn't go to school here. But get real — he's a teacher!"

That night, however, Sam Braverman called his best friend back in Boston. "You wouldn't believe this girl if you met her," he said. "She seems so much older than seventeen. She reads Hegel and Marx and Faulkner and Joyce. I lent her Kozinsky's *The Painted Bird*, and she read that, too. I can't stop myself. I love talking to her — she's more fun than anyone else here. "But you know how I feel — it's highly irresponsible to date students, even immoral. This whole situation stinks."

Nina Curtin and Sam Braverman remained friends for six months before they admitted how they felt about each other. Nina, who had started calling him Sam, would tease him. She complained that, when they were together, he'd go into "teacher mode." "All of a sudden, out of nowhere, you become awfully formal, Sam. You start treating me like a student or a proctee, instead of a friend."

Finally, Sam Braverman blurted out: "How do you expect me to treat you? If I were to pretend that you weren't a student, I might say something I shouldn't."

"Like what?" Nina inquired calmly. Inside she was about to explode.

"This is completely off the record, Nina. But, the fact is, that under different circumstances, I would like to go out with you."

Nina couldn't sleep all night. She was thrilled, incredulous. She was also a little frightened. So many times, she had imagined a conversation like this, planned it out in her head. Now that it had been spoken in reality, the words seemed strange, brash.

Initially, Sam and Nina decided they would wait until her high school graduation before becoming physically involved. A week later, however, they kissed in Sam's room. For the first time all year, Sam closed his door and locked it. He didn't want any of his proctees to come in.

Sam made Nina promise not to tell anyone, "not even your roommates," he insisted. "I know they're trustworthy, but once you tell one person, the story always get out."

Nina kept quiet, so quiet that Susanna and Claire grew puzzled. Why had Nina stopped talking about Mr.Braverman all of a sudden? And she started getting weekend passes "to see friends of the family," as she put it. "You don't know them," she assured them.

Sam and Nina went for drives in New England. They went to Boston to the Commons and the galleries on Newbury Street. They went to Amherst and visited Emily Dickinson's house. At school, Nina grew increasingly private and secretive. She avoided friends and couldn't concentrate on her work. She got a C on a French test. All she could think about was Sam, and there was no one she could tell. The relationship absorbed her entirely. It swallowed her up.

When spring vacation came, Nina told her parents she had to stay in school for a couple of extra days to finish a paper. In truth, she had planned a private weekend with Sam at his house in western Massachusetts. Nina had convinced herself that at last she was ready to sleep with him. It would be her first time.

Nina returned from spring vacation visibly upset. She avoided Sam when she could; a simple "hello" from him in the dining hall was enough to leave her shaken. Growing increasingly worried, Sam insisted they meet and talk. Nina finally agreed. But once she was face to face with him, Nina was unable to look him in the eye. She squirmed when he tried to touch her. Repeatedly, Sam asked her what was wrong. Nina said she didn't know.

Nina's roommates became concerned. Nina wasn't sleeping more than three hours a night, and she avoided going to meals. She was losing weight, and she looked tired and drawn. Nina was distraught about something, and Susanna and Claire suspected what it might be. Finally, they went to their proctor in Barrow House. They described Nina's behavior and what they thought was the cause.

Nina was surprised when she was summoned to meet with Louisa Burnside, the Dean of Girls. Mrs. Burnside asked Nina directly about her relationship with Sam Braverman. The matter had been brought to her attention by Nina's proctor, she said.

Faced with the question, Nina answered openly. Mrs. Burnside met with Nina three more times, to learn the full circumstances and to assure the girl that she would not get in trouble. When the administration spoke to Sam as well, he admitted that Nina's story was true.

The staff discussed the case and decided that Sam Braverman must be dismissed. It was already May, the dean told Sam, so he would stay the remainder of the term. But his contract would not be renewed for the following year.

Nina and Sam did not talk much during the rest of the spring term. When Nina graduated, Sam wished her good luck. He gave her a collection of Yeats' poetry with a note inside. The next fall, Nina began her freshman year at Yale. She hasn't heard from Sam since.

The friendship that existed between Nina Curtin and Sam Braverman was strong and genuine, as was the attraction. Sam resisted a relationship with Nina as long as he felt he could. Eventually, however, their friendship became so intense that the barriers that separated them as student and mentor seemed to dissolve. Sam thought that Nina was more mature than other girls her age, mature enough to grapple with the problems of an illicit relationship at her school.

But although Nina was mature intellectually, she was naive sexually. Initially, she was awed by Sam. She found his professional inaccessibility impressive, attractive. In addition, she needed a mature friend as a role model, as a guide. Dating him was a dream which she never expected to come true. When it did, she was excited but confused. She adored and admired Sam, but she wasn't prepared for a concrete physical relationship with him. The final experience of sleeping with Sam left Nina feeling inexplicably upset, violated.

Besides, the relationship was fraught with the kind of worry that few seventeen-year-olds have to encounter. For months, Nina had been investing more and more of her emotional energy in her relationship with Sam. She had no outlet to express her feelings; instead, she became isolated, detached from the rest of the campus community. The final disclosure of the affair, although a shock, was a relief to Nina as well.

The power structure at prep schools is highly stratified. Authority, academic and disciplinary, rests with the members of the faculty, while the student body must respect and obey them. The contract that binds both sides is a paradoxical one. The obedience the students show their teachers enables the teachers to serve the students, to supply them with the academic preparation they need for college.

Teachers are urged not to take advantage of the power inherent in their position. Students should feel that their superiors are consistent and fair; that the policy directed toward any one of them will automatically apply to all. Teachers must follow the rules of the institution.

But in the high-powered, close-knit community of a boarding school, strong bonds develop between teacher and student. When personal-professional barriers begin to break down, as they did with Sam and Nina, with Belinda and Josh, it grows increasingly difficult to set limits on intimacy. A teacher becomes a confidante and friend — why not a lover? Ultimately, however, most student-teacher relationships have unfortunate results. Apart from breaking the rules of their community, they usually end by hurting the individuals involved.

It is easier to maintain distance at a day school, where the teachers need only perform in the classroom. What happens behind the scenes — domestically, romantically — remains a mystery. At a boarding school, however, privacy is hard to come by. Students and teachers see each other all the time — not only in the classroom and dorm, but at the swimming pool and on the squash courts, at campus movies and student-faculty talent shows.

As resident counselors, teachers feel empathy for their students, compassion for the struggles they must face growing up away from home. The prep school campus is a microcosm of the outside world. Every mood swing — whether the panic of an academic crisis, the euphoria of an athletic success, or the manic obsession of a teenage crush — is magnified, causes tremors. Such tremors shake teachers as well.

15

Beating the System

by Stan Creek

The purpose of house faculty in boarding schools is to serve as parents of the students who attend the institution. As would-be-parents, the school sets social and moral guidelines for its "children." In most parent/adolescent relationships, the adolescent tests limits and defies his parents' edicts. The resulting behavior in boarding schools is often more extreme than at home because it is so much more difficult to supervise such a large "family."

One of the most popular ways to break the rules is known as "cruising" — sneaking out of the dorm after curfew. The first time I cruised was during my sophomore year. A couple of friends and I and our female counterparts plotted for weeks how we would go about getting away with it. We conversed in the smoking areas during our free periods, and after a lot of thought, came up with a plan. First, we had to make sure we had access to the girls' dorm. This detail was left to the ladies, who decided they would wait until their dorm proctors were securely behind the doors of their private apartments, to make sure the front door was left open. In case it was somehow discovered and relocked, the back-up plan involved leaving the living room window open to crawl through. Our part was the risky half. We had to somehow dodge the patrolling security guards and make it to the ladies' dorm without either being detected absent from our own dorms or entering another dorm after curfew. Actually, it was easier than we anticipated. For one thing, when eleven o'clock came, time for lights-out, the dorm proctors usually would not make contact again until morning except in an emergency such as a fire drill.

As far as successfully navigating a safe path to the women's dormitory, that was surprisingly easy. The whereabouts of the security guards were very predictable for anyone who took the time to notice, and we did. We tracked their patrol for a week and consulted upperclassmen on the subject. Finally, we constructed a chart which pinpointed the guards' various positions on campus all during the night. As a result, we made it to the women's dorm with no problem. Once inside, things went very smoothly. Our women lived in an isolated corner of the top floor, so we had all the privacy we needed. After a few glasses of vodka and orange juice supplied by the ladies, the evening progressed into sexual play, interrupted only by the fact that we had to return to our dorm rooms before daylight so as not to tip off our "parents" as to our actions.

As the years went on, our sneaking-out activities became increasingly complex; we even got to the point where we did not have to return to our dorms before daybreak. We devised ways around it, secrets only we knew, handed down to us and handed down by us to the class below.

Another way to beat the system was to purchase and consume alcohol without being discovered by the dorm faculty. We would frequently go into town during the week and have someone of legal age buy for us. We'd bring the liquor back to school and hide it in our rooms — in the closets, in suitcases under the bed, or in the dressers in our clothes until the weekend when we'd consume it. Since it was too risky to drink in the dorms, we usually got a group of friends together and snuck away to the local graveyard where we proceeded to get intoxicated.

While getting drunk in the graveyard and returning to our dorms without getting caught was fun, what really gave us a thrill was to engage in sexual play where adults least expected it, in the classrooms. This usually took a lot of planning and some luck. Once a girl I had been seeing and I tried it. Our plan was simple but very effective. First, we made sure we only used the classrooms farthest from the flow of traffic; then we made sure we used them only in the early morning before breakfast or late evening after study hall but before check-in. This way, we always had the rooms to ourselves and never had to worry about anyone interrupting us.

During the school day, when the classrooms were not available, my friends and I became more creative. Once I was in French class sitting next to a girl I was attracted to. We starting flirting innocently while class was in session. She would gently brush against my thigh and write very suggestive notes. Not to be outdone, I did the same in return with each note becoming more and more explicit. By the end of class, it was obvious I had become quite flustered, but to my pleasant surprise, so had the young lady. As we both had a free block that period, we decided we would try to ease each other's sexual frustrations. Since classes were still in session, we couldn't use the classrooms, and the dormitories were locked until classes were over. The solution came in the form of the junior class cubby area, which at the time was still under construction, but had lots of little rooms which provided enough space for two and still afforded privacy from anyone who might happen to wander by. Once we were securely in the room, we acted out some of the suggestions we had written earlier in our notes. However, since neither of us had protection, we kept our play to an acceptable minimum.

Classrooms and cubby areas were not the only places for sexual play on the school grounds. Once a girlfriend of mine was in a school play and had to spend all her evenings rehearsing. I figured I wouldn't be able to see her for a couple of months; I was wrong. As things turned out, I was introduced to another part of the school which was perfect for private sexual play, the music rooms in the theatrical wing. We were guaranteed to find free space since her breaks came at that time in the evening when study hall was just ending; everyone would either be rushing downtown or to the smoking pit before curfew. So, whenever she had some free time we would meet in one of the free rooms, lock the door, and usually end up petting heavily, often performing oral sex.

Another area on campus, which was used quite often and which didn't take much planning, was the chapel. It was a place of assembly, however, it doubled as a place used by couples at night to satisfy their sexual desires. I was introduced to the chapel as an intimate place by a girl I had been seeing off and on during my entire boarding school career. It was one of her fantasies to make love in the chapel. When she told me this, I was more than happy to oblige her. However, the planning for this one became a little tricky because the only good time to use the chapel for such a purpose was when most everyone could be accounted for, thus assuring no unwanted guests. Since we were both upperclassmen and not required to attend study hall, we decided this would be the best time to fulfill her fantasy. When study hall started, we both ventured over to the chapel, separately, so as not to cause any suspicion. Since the entrance was always left open, getting in was no problem, but to be on the safe side, we decided it would be best to use one of the balconies just in case someone else was to visit. Adding a little excitement to the evening's exercise was the fact that right in the middle of our actions, a couple of teachers came in and sat down to talk on the first level. We made love straight through their conversation. The fact that we were able to get away with doing it while two teachers were in the same room made the whole thing even more enjoyable. It was like having your cake and eating it too. In fact, to this day, whenever I run into this particular young lady, we always reflect on that evening.

Other places where rules were broken were at parties and on school trips. Even though chaperones were present, they couldn't keep their eyes on everyone. A classic example was the time one of my friends on the soccer team threw a party. While the chaperones did do an exceptional job patrolling the party within the house, they forgot all about the backyard. But a lady friend and I did not. We casually slipped away, separately of course, and met outside. There, we found the tool shed and let nature take its course. However, at most of these parties, a little planning did go into where and with whom we would finally end up sleeping. Usually the day before the party, an unofficial list of rooms available for couples to use would be circulated by those who planned the bash. I remember one party where only ten people were invited, the sole purpose being to party together and eventually end up in bed. The organization was brilliant. I got together with four friends and divided the responsibilities. One person was in charge of securing the booze, another a house, another protection, and last, but not least, the women. We chose women we knew were most likely to be agreeable to our suggestions. We planned the whole thing to happen on a long weekend, when we knew we would be free to leave the campus for an extended period of time without having to go home to our respective parents. We all falsified our permission slips, ended up at my friend's parents' weekend home, and proceeded to have quite an uninhibited weekend.

Another example was on my junior class trip. Months before, I had plotted with my classmates ways to smuggle drugs on this trip. A friend of mine and his girl friend came up with a foolproof plan for sneaking their pot and cocaine in the girl's tampon case. Not one chaperone ever thought of checking there. While it was easy to sneak the drugs, securing alcohol was another story. When we arrived at the trip site, I took a cab with a couple of friends to the hotel. We paid the driver to buy for us and gave him instructions on how to get the alcohol to us. First, he was to let us off at our hotel; then, he was to go to the store and buy the liquor; finally, we designated the bushes in back of the hotel as the drop point. The whole thing worked like a charm, and the weekend turned into one big alcohol and drugfest. The thing which saved any one of us from being singled out for disciplinary action was that everyone was involved, so no one could point fingers. But, because we were eventually found out, future class trips were forbidden. My classmates and I became legends to the younger students, however, since we had been able to pull off such a stunt.

While parties and class trips offered the perfect environment for getting around rules, there also existed some very unlikely places which were just as good. The most memorable was at another school after one of my basketball games. Because of scheduling problems, the varsity team played before the junior varsity. When our game was over, we had to stick around and wait for the J.V. team since we shared the same bus. On this particular trip, we had some female spectators from our school accompany us. One was a girl I had been flirting with for some time. As fate would have it, this young lady and I decided to take a walk around the school grounds instead of watching the J.V. game. As we walked, we talked about our feelings for each other and decided we would give a relationship a chance. On the trip back to school, we sat in the back of the bus together. We knew this section would provide us with the most privacy from faculty and students. Our trip home was filled with lots of kissing and touching. This close contact made us both horny, so in order to satisfy ourselves, I asked two teammates sitting in front of us to serve as a barrier from the faculty in the front of the bus. They agreed, and my new girl friend and I proceeded to please each other. We sat very close, arm in arm, with our jackets draped over ourselves. This way, no one could see what we were doing. By this time, most of the people on the bus were either asleep or busily talking to the person next to them. Also the fact that the bus was not lit, and it was now dark outside, gave us perfect cover. With these factors in our favor, she pretended to be sleeping in my lap. Again, we used our coats as cover while she fulfilled my request.

The one episode in my boarding school days, which tops all others as far as sexual play right under the nose of the faculty, happened to my roommate senior year. It took place in a faculty member's home. A friend of ours was going to be baby-sitting there on a particular Friday night. Since I was already in a serious relationship but my roommate was not, we went right to work setting up a plan for him. First, we made sure the young lady would go for the idea of becoming intimate with him. She and I had a close friendship and were able to talk about anything, so I confronted her with it. After her involvement was secured, we went over the plan for her to call us as soon as the faculty member and his wife had left the house. The call came, and we went over. The purpose of my being there was to keep an eye on the child while she and my roommate had sex in the faculty member's bed. When we got there, she had already put the child to sleep, so all I had to do was watch the kid and keep a lookout to make sure the parents did not come home early. Everything went as planned, but they left a tremendous stain on the sheet. To this day, I don't know how she explained that one.

As far as outright disregard for school rules while in the presence of faculty, nothing beats our class play the day before graduation. While rehearsing in front of a faculty member and performing the first show for the parents and faculty, we followed the school guidelines. However, for the second show, meant only for underclassmen, we agreed among ourselves to be as delinquent as we could get away with, and then some. So we held back nothing. In the scene which called for alcohol use, we used real alcohol; in the scene which called for drug use, we used real drugs; in the scenes which called for sex, we were not shy. The only reason we were able to get away with this was that, except in a few blatant scenes, the audience, which included some faculty members, believed we were acting. It wasn't until after graduation that the faculty got wind of the real story. Because of that second play, the classes which followed us had to adhere to more stringent rules.

In short, even though the faculty of our institution tried its best to keep us from engaging in acts contrary to suggested guidelines, the fact remains that we developed numerous schemes to get around their rules. It was just in our nature as young adults to try and circumvent their authority. While our actions might have been juvenile and uncalled for, those incidents in our boarding career were essential for our preparation for college. While the school prepared us academically, our constant endeavors to beat the system helped us prepare for college social life. While most freshmen spent the first semester of their college careers trying to find themselves emotionally and get used to living with other people their own age, we already had a good idea who we were and how to deal with a crowd of peers because of those incidents and the resulting camaraderie from boarding school. Essentially, our desire to beat the system was just another rite of passage as young adults, a rite which gave us a head start socially when we entered college.

16

Emerging into the Outside World

by A.H. Glass

After graduating from prep school, my impression of distance between the prep environment and the real world was erased. School boundaries no longer sheltered; school rules no longer regulated; the people around me no longer shared my beliefs; and some resented the very idea of prep school and the Old Boy network.

The lip service students pay to ideals at prep school withers against naked reality: the experience of intolerance. Exposure to people whose beliefs and backgrounds are threatening is unquestionably rewarding, but prep school did not prepare me for it. Some of the reasons are inherent in the practice of closing off a group of children of mostly similar backgrounds and high test scores from the environment at large. A student may be prepared for academics, honor and success, but not for the flood of diversity that anyone with a healthy curiosity will find outside prep culture.

Some cope with the prep school experience by remaining comfortably within prep networks that arise after graduation. This includes choosing to go to an Ivy League college, seeking one's friends from among the preps, joining exclusive clubs or fraternities. After college, nothing provides a better example than returning to live and work at one's alma mater, though the support systems fostered beyond school can be just as insulating as remaining within its walls. In fact, because the network is an invisible structure, it can be harder to transcend than returning to school, where some go back specifically to address this problem.

Two or three teachers at my prep school worked as hard at shaking up our complacency and challenging our values as at developing our skills in English, Math, or Latin. Although rare, these were the real teachers, for they reached past the curriculum into our lives. One teacher in particular stood out in my time at prep school. He taught English, Geometry, Latin, and Logic; he played concert piano and held several state track and field records; he had written books on Greek mythology and English grammar as well as on the pitfalls of imprecise thought. Intensity and clarity marked his classes, and only the most callous failed to learn from him. I wish I could have found more such teachers; they encounter only a few students each year and get through to even less. Conversely, the students who shuffle through school and into the networks of college and career have little to guard themselves against people or events that undermine their beliefs, nothing save their own insularity. For that life, prep school fulfills its role well.

The diversity I encountered at college was enough to shake the assumption that I had been well prepared by my prep school. The scorn and derision of those who succeeded without the helping hand of prep school could be sharp. I distinctly remember my freshman writing course where everyone had equal ability but drew on radically different experiences. The three of us who had attended prep school often wrote of our lives there, unconsciously reflecting the values born of prep culture. In doing so, we drew some severe and belittling comments, not necessarily on what we wrote but on the attitude we brought to our subjects. It was not arrogance, but a complacency of ideals, ideals which we had rarely tested against experience. That one class taught me more than all of prep school about the often subtle forms of racism and sexism, the range of attitudes toward sexual behavior, the political agendas of both extremes, and the right of each person to believe in the supremacy of his own experience.

When you meet people whose worlds threaten yours, you either become silent and doubting, or aggressive and unyielding. In our class, the three of us from prep schools tended to hold together and support each other's opinions. Not until later in college did I learn to accept criticism of my beliefs, to acknowledge that a thoughtless remark may have contained an implicit slur or bias, and to try to adjust my view of the world when the experience of others was more convincing than my own. None of this would have been possible had I not found my close friends outside the prep school network and left the latter to support my acquaintances.

Prep school graduates who seek contact with other corners of American culture often face confusion and hostility, but ultimately gain a broad and deep understanding from experiences that force questioning prep school ideals, that demand to be reconciled with the way prep school teaches things "should be." Many of the great successes born of the prep culture, including a large number of presidents and government officials, have had to make their mark outside that sphere, notably in war and public service, before being accepted by the world at large.

The privilege of prep school often feels like a handicap, and anyone who has tried to reach beyond the prep culture knows the stigma that can attend you. I know one alumnus of prep school and an Ivy League college who, with the privileges of wealth behind him and the usual array of careers before him, joined the Marines. The reaction of his friends struck me most: disbelief that he would choose to put himself where the advantages of an elite education would work against him. "Pretty brave;" "Think of the hazing he'll get," his friends all said. These comments show that most prep school students had shared a part of what was in store for their friend. At most universities, prep school students are a small minority, privileged, often visible, and distant from others. The animosity bred at prep school between the preps and the local public school students often translates into either reserve or spite at college based on the fear encountered earlier in the insularity of prep school. Only for a few is the prep school disposition arrogance; for most, it is born of the herd instinct and the habit of at least four years of a secluded existence.

One of the strengths and flaws of prep school is that it supports a privileged minority. The strength of privilege is not just in training or in mere wealth, but in the opportunities one has as part of a network of peers and elders who achieve and help their own to achieve in business, government, or the arts. The flaw is that it teaches by example to uphold an American aristocracy despite the abundance of liberal minds running the schools. The stress on gamesmanship, tradition, exclusive education, and the glory of school history leads to an environment where involvement in issues of poverty and intolerance becomes a question of noblesse oblige. The hands stay clean, the chin held high, the house secure, the garden trimmed.

Charity, even from a distance, should inspire admiration, and prep school definitely teaches the doctrine, "From those to whom much is given, much is expected." Prep schools try to teach generosity of spirit, even if only some learn it, so it is no surprise to find prep school successes helping others later on. But, in the process of attaining success, the prep alumnus finds the world may not play by his rules linking good contacts with nepotism. Broader society won't uphold values inherited from the prep environment, and may hold in contempt a prep-inspired system of charity. I suppose it is because we learn to help ourselves before helping others.

One way in which my prep school experience was probably similar to most was that, although I didn't like my time there, in retrospect, I am glad I went. At least prep school teaches a balance of conservative and liberal ideals, and it prepares one to be intellectually open-minded. The problems of testing that open-mindedness against experience and charges of naivete are up to the individual. I believe my school did the best it could with its structure and the aristocratic baggage it passed onto us, which we carry around afterward, consciously or not. Unfortunately, many prep schools teach their students to be proud of their school, its renown for excellence and ancestral traditions, rather than to be modest about the opportunities it offers, however imperfect the overall education may have been. I wonder if the discrepancy between that pride and the imperfection of what prep schools have to offer is the source of animosity that many students develop towards their school. They are persuaded to believe in its glory and become bitter when they discover its flaws.

For me, the hassles of going to a prep school and of encountering a world hostile to its elitist reputation were more than compensated for by the intellectual environment of which most prep schools have a right to be proud. Once one has gained the desire to step outside the network, one need only patience and flexibility to receive the embrace of those whose opinions differ.

Conclusion:

Toward A Solution

by Louis M. Crosier

Student reactions to boarding school are seldom neutral. This is not surprising given the ingredients that go into the experience. The rigorous daily academic schedule and the nightly campus-wide slumber party are directly at odds. This results in considerable sustained pressure on the students — some as young as thirteen — who must choose between discipline and experimentation, and who often get torn apart trying to do it all. The combination of the emotional volatility characteristic of adolescence and the accessibility of so much opportunity can make boarding school an overwhelming place. What's missing from the experience is adequate guidance in learning to make healthy choices and avoid self-defeating behavior. Adults in the boarding community can be valuable in this regard because they have had more practice doing just that. Unfortunately, their time is in short supply.

Prep school students are at greater risk than necessary. They differ from students who go to public high schools or private day schools because they don't see their parents each night and they don't leave their peers. As a result, they bond very closely with the other students and have less interaction with adults than they would at home. This lack of adult contact leads to perhaps the greatest flaw in residential schooling: the children parent themselves.

Students quickly learn they must tend to their own health, set their own limits, and reward themselves. They realize that within the extensive list of rules, there is a great deal of freedom. Although prep school offers little privacy from peers, it is easy for students to go unnoticed by adults. One or two residential faculty members cannot possibly keep track of an entire dormitory of kids. More significantly, the residential faculty cannot spend quality time with each student on a regular basis. All the little things that a parent does at home — asking how school went or saying "good night" before bed — let the child know that someone cares. Despite residential faculty members' hard work and good intentions, boarders do not get enough of their attention.

A certain number of faculty members at boarding schools live in the dormitory apartments as part of their role in the community. In addition to teaching and often coaching, Residence Hall Director is one of many "hats" faculty members wear during the course of a normal day, but it is not viewed as the primary responsibility. At a day school, the day ends when the kids go home after sports. At prep school, the school day can be divided into two parts: the academic and the residential. The academic day includes classes and athletics; the residential day begins in the late afternoon when the students return from sports to prepare for dinner, study hall, and the evening rituals of visiting, socializing, and doing homework. Since the tight academic schedule is over, students assume added responsibility for their time. In addition to any structured evening events, there are several hours of free time before bed and many hours after "bedtime." Even if "lights-out" is required, it is hard to enforce this rule. Nights can provide a long and active hidden curriculum.

Prep schools allocate most of their resources to the academic portion of the day. Thus they produce cognitively sophisticated students whose social and emotional development have been left relatively unattended. While this does not engender emotional disaster, it does put students at risk. Prep schools have the resources to create a more balanced experience for their students, but will have to make the decision to realign fundamental priorities to achieve this end. Herein lies the challenge which will distinguish the best boarding schools in the next decade, as parents realize prep schools are often ill equipped to meet the needs of kids in an increasingly complex society.

What the Schools Can Do

Change the Priorities: The Job in the Dorm Should be Number One

The job description of the residential faculty needs to be revised so that parental duties take precedence over academic responsibilities. In other words, boarding faculty should begin their work day just before dinner. They would then be fresh and prepared to handle a dorm of adolescents returning from a full day of success and failure in the classroom and on the playing field. This is the time kids process the day's events; most student "crises" occur after the sun goes down. Students do not want to come back to a dorm where the adult in charge is as tired as they are. They need someone to welcome them "home," to ask how their day has been, to listen and take an interest in them.

Faculty members also need to process their day when they return from work. They do not feel like opening their apartment to twenty teenagers after spending the previous nine hours with them. They need to relax and be with their families. It is too much to ask for professionalism from a faculty member eighteen hours a day.

Thus, the school must view the job of running a dorm as important, which means more than giving the concept lip service. Residential faculty need to be paid a full salary for their work in the dorms. They need a detailed job description complete with expectations, training and regular evaluations. Prep schools are not known for holding their faculty accountable outside the classroom. As in all schools, autonomy is a sacred element of teaching, and accountability is often misconstrued as interference. In addition, since residential faculty usually have more jobs than they can reasonably handle, their supervisors hesitate to confront them. Thus, mediocrity in residential life is self-perpetuating, and the problem of having an unrealistic quantity of work is not effectively addressed. Students in the dorms will continue to receive inadequate attention and supervision until schools value the job of residential faculty as much as that of classroom teacher.

Change the Structure: Reallocate Resources to Ensure Quality Adult Presence

Having adults on campus does not guarantee their presence will be felt. They need to interact with students to have an impact on them. Children need adults who have time and care enough about them to help them appreciate their self-worth and impress upon them their ability to have a positive impact on the world. They need adults who will set limits and provide for contingencies, present challenges, encourage success and lend support in the case of failure. Even though teenagers may feign deafness, they pay very close attention to adults.

Any number of people can provide students with the kind of relationship normally associated with a parent, but the job is probably best done by the natural parents; they know the child, have a personal stake in his success and have already experienced challenges and dilemmas which are specific to the child's background. Residence hall directors assume the challenge of raising children who are not their own. In fact, they are called on to monitor the development of twenty or more teenagers at once.

Either the number of adults on campus whose job is to tend to the affective needs of boarding students needs to grow, or the amount of quality time every adult can spend in casual contact with the students needs to increase. Both are acceptable and both are possible. However, boarding schools work with a finite amount of resources, so a shift will have to occur. Some area of the school curriculum will have to change to allow for improvement in the residential program. Given the importance of the boarding program and the extent to which it has been neglected at most schools in the past, it seems reasonable to consider reallocating existing resources. This means diverting a portion of the budget to residential life or reducing the load of the dorm faculty by cutting courses from the curriculum or by hiring additional non-residential teachers to take on some of the teaching load. In addition, launching an aggressive capital campaign earmarked to endow improvements in the residential curriculum would be appropriate.

The Time Dividend: Ten Steps Forward

Increasing the amount of time adults in the dorms have to focus on their students would increase their effectiveness in many ways.

First, residential faculty members could keep a dorm log containing a brief summary of each evening's events including any significant incidents. This they would pass to the person on duty on any given night. A log of this nature allows for consistency between proctors and a way to keep communication current and professional. Documentation is an efficient way to trace student's behavioral trends. It promotes effective follow-up on the previous day's events by each proctor and keeps the faculty role in the dorm continuous rather than fragmented.

Second, at the beginning of the term, the dorm faculty could call each child's parents to introduce themselves, be available for questions and be inquisitive about any idiosyncrasies about which they should know in order to help make the child's boarding experience more positive. Speaking with parents not only helps provide helpful background information about students and their home situation, but also opens the lines of communication between home and school. The more known about each student, the easier it is to connect with him and his family.

Third, residence hall directors would be able to use their additional time to plan dorm activities. Small group activities and events involving the entire dorm create spirit and a sense of belonging to a community. They also provide an opportunity for the dorm director to see the kids interact and help integrate students who are having trouble finding their niche.

Fourth, residential faculty members would have time during the school day to contact teachers and guidance counselors to discuss students about whom they have concerns. These meetings would allow time to put together all the pieces on individuals who might otherwise slip through the cracks.

Fifth, weekly gatherings of the entire boarding faculty could provide a time to discuss issues pertaining to the whole community. Topics for discussion could be very specific and might include sensitive issues such as: 1) What to do when a house parent comes across two students having intercourse — What if they are of the same sex and in the same dorm? 2) What to do when the dorm proctor runs across a kid throwing up in the bathroom? Is he sick; has he been drinking; is he anorexic/bulimic? 3) How to deal with a student's personal tragedy such as a death in the family? 4) How to get kids to go to bed earlier; what to do about late night noise in the dorm? 5) What to do if a student is frequently sick: is he eating properly, getting enough sleep, doing drugs? In essence, residential faculty would have time to discuss all the challenges they might encounter while running a dorm and come up with appropriate solutions for their schools. Other less urgent, yet important, topics could include issues of repair and maintenance, coordination of traditions and all-campus activities, questions of consistency and accountability. These meetings could serve as an opportunity to create a strong sense of community and camaraderie among faculty.

Sixth, residential faculty could attend all meals and campus events. Meals provide another opportunity for faculty to interact with students and notice whether or not the kids are eating well and cultivating healthy relationships and attitudes. Faculty could sit with a group of students rather than with faculty at a separate table and could be there at the beginning of meals and leave with the last students. This would not be unreasonable if it is considered part of their job and occurred during their working hours. Students have ample time to spend with each other on their own, so whenever students and faculty are in the same place, the two groups should be integrated.

Seventh, cutting the teaching and extra duty load of residential faculty members would allow time and energy to hold the kids in the dorms accountable for dorm responsibilities and inappropriate behavior. Currently, students often get away with a lot because house faculty simply don't have the energy to play the "heavy." Instead of effective ways to work through problems, faculty often rely on threats and unreasonable punishment to shape student behavior. When tired and rushed, it is easy to find fault with children's actions and hard to appreciate what they have done well. If house faculty have more time and energy, the quality of their interaction with the students will be better and the chances of creating strong relationships will increase.

Eighth, there could be meetings between residential faculty of different schools. There could be more communication between schools concerning alternative ways to handle different situations in the dorm. Conferences of several days during the winter and over spring break would encourage group problem solving. Schools that have already confronted and dealt with a complicated situation could share ideas with those who might be searching for solutions to a similar issue.

Ninth, more time would mean more opportunities for casual conversation and informal student contact. Small group activities within the dorm such as fireside chats with tea and hot chocolate, or playing basketball or board games give students a chance to get to know one another and faculty an opportunity to build strong relationships with the kids. Faculty should help students with their homework and study skills; they should take an interest in what the kids are learning and validate its importance. An open door when on duty is a nice way of letting the kids know they are welcome and can come seek help, advice or conversation. Faculty should walk around the dorm regularly to see how the kids are doing. They should not hesitate to let students know that the reason they are walking around is to talk to them and see how they are doing. Initially, students may think faculty are patrolling because they don't trust the kids, but in time they will appreciate the genuine interest. All these seemingly small gestures help create a more open environment of mutual respect in the dorm.

Finally, an additional way to increase the feeling of adult presence at prep school would be to pair students with local alumnae/i and day student families. This works well if the school has a substantial day student population or an active alumnae/i body in the area. If using external constituencies is impossible, a limited community family hosting system could be set up for students particularly in need of adult support or for international students and those who live long distances from home. The family hosts would have the student over for an occasional weekend, a meal, or take him off campus for an afternoon as a change of scene. Creating a feeling of family outside the school will only help the kids feel valued even more than they do as a result of competent faculty parenting.

House faculty do not have the time to take the steps toward creating a healthy positive living environment when they have to prepare for a full load of classes and coaching. It is too much to ask, but too important to forego. Since the kids are away from their parents, the job of the residential faculty is to fill that role as well as possible. The current structure of most prep schools reflects a gross underestimation of the importance and the demands of running a residence hall which serves the best interests of teenagers.

Change the Foundation: Hiring and Training

Who are the adults who run the dorms? They are generally people who join the faculty to teach, but are willing to take on a dorm job as well. Often they accept the dormitory responsibilities because the "free housing" is very appealing. If you ask members of the residential faculty why they live in the dorm, it is unlikely that you find many who feel it is an opportunity to build kids' self-esteem and help them learn to live a healthy, well-rounded life. Thus, prep school faculty members understand that they have duties in addition to teaching, but they feel their primary responsibility is in the classroom. Their expertise is teaching; most learn how to run a dorm by doing it.

Dorm faculty come in lots of different shapes and sizes — experienced, inexperienced, married and single, with and without children. Each of these family configurations has its advantages and its limitations. But all residential faculty have two things in common: first, they all have personal lives, a need for privacy, and a need to have a distance from their work on a regular basis. Second, none of them knows anything more than any other about running a dorm of adolescent children before they have actually done it. One might argue that a couple who has had their own teenagers might have a better understanding of the kids; or, a young faculty member who had recently been a teenager might identify with students better than an older faculty member. But, as the essays in the book would suggest, the combination of putting a group of kids in a small, insulated living environment with extensive rules, pressures and expectations, yields behaviors and networks that are not altogether predictable. Even a person with extensive experience with adolescents is not prepared for the unique group dynamic which results from such a situation. Unless faculty members have received training specifically designed to prepare them to live in a dorm, they will not be ready to deal with the unexpected, and a good portion of what goes on in the dorm will remain unknown to them.

A background in crisis management, adolescent counseling, substance abuse and adolescent sexuality is helpful. In addition, house faculty need to be familiar with their school's procedures for dealing with emergencies of all types. It is not enough to know that if there is an "emergency," the response is to call a certain number.

There are many conferences and workshops dealing with topics related to running a residence hall. Educational organizations, hospitals, and therapy centers throughout the United States offer these kinds of opportunities on a regular basis. For additional information, call The National Association of Independent Schools (NAIS) or The Independent School Association of Massachusetts (ISAM). The issues covered at these events include topics such as: creating a chemical free community, men running girls' dorms, senior and new faculty mentor relationships, and financial planning for career educators. The National Endowment for the Humanities (NEH) and other foundations and government groups offer research grants related to education. The Dean of Residential Life at each prep school should provide his staff with conference listings, and the schools should pay for any interested teachers to attend the workshops. In many cases, prep schools already do this. In addition, schools should hold regular "in-service" workshops to address issues of particular relevance to the school and encourage ongoing self-evaluation and improvement.

It is in the community's best interest to closely examine the process for hiring faculty who live in dorms. Those already in dorms who are there for the wrong reasons should be removed, and all residential faculty should be trained and should continue to add to their resources. There are many opportunities to make the dorm living easier for the residential faculty and more beneficial for the students.

Putting all the pieces together, you get a portrait of overextended faculty members (many of whom are inexperienced) raising twenty or more teenagers who have strong incentive to avoid healthy behavior and honest dialogue with adults. Add academic pressure, fatigue, and a lot of fun distractions, and it becomes clear the non-academic side of prep school needs attention. As we move into the '90s, it will be even more essential to reevaluate the residential programs of our prep schools, building on existing strengths, reallocating resources and weeding out burnt-out faculty rather than patching holes with traditional Band-Aids. While the student subculture will remain strong at boarding school, perhaps schools can catch more kids before they fall through the cracks as casualties of privilege.